WOULD YOU DO THAT TO YOUR MOTHER?

Also by Jeanne Bliss

CHIEF CUSTOMER OFFICER:
Getting Past Lip Service to Passionate Action

I LOVE YOU MORE THAN MY DOG:
Five Decisions That Drive Extreme Customer Loyalty
in Good Times and Bad

CHIEF CUSTOMER OFFICER 2.0:
How to Build Your Customer-Driven Growth Engine

WOULD YOU DO THAT TO YOUR MOTHER?

The "Make Mom Proud" Standard
for How to Treat Your Customers

JEANNE BLISS

PORTFOLIO / PENGUIN

Portfolio/Penguin
An imprint of Penguin Random House LLC
375 Hudson Street
New York, New York 10014

Most Portfolio books are available at a discount when purchased in quantity for sales promotions or corporate use. Special editions, which include personalized covers, excerpts, and corporate imprints, can be created when purchased in large quantities. For more information, please call (212) 572-2232 or email specialmarkets@penguinrandomhouse.com. Your local bookstore can also assist with discounted bulk purchases using the Penguin Random House corporate Business-to-Business program. For assistance in locating a participating retailer, email B2B@penguinrandomhouse.com.

ISBN: 9780735217812 (hardcover)
ISBN: 9780735217829 (ebook)

Printed in the United States of America
1   3   5   7   9   10   8   6   4   2

Designed by Laura K. Corless
Set in New Caledonia LT Std

For moms,
who nudge us toward becoming
the best version of ourselves

Contents

1.

Picture Your Mom.

Our childhood. Mom's lessons. And our business life.
They share freely. They have our back. They are there, in good times and bad. They always have our best interest in mind. They are brave.

This describes our moms.

It also describes companies that <u>follow her lead</u> in how they grow their businesses.

The lessons we learned as kids stick with us. And often they have our mom's face all over them. Her guidance, her rules, and her sayings are still in our heads. You probably grew up that way too, with a simple, clear understanding of what to do and what not to do.

We were taught to share, trust each other, play nice in the sandbox, and treat others like we'd want to be treated. Those lessons remain some of the best advice we've ever been given.

They also remain some of our most sound advice for how to behave in business.

Companies that **"Make Mom Proud"** grow by *living* those lessons. They remove practices that might curb the extension of care, or limit employees to act in good conscience. They work to remove boundaries and pressures that prohibit customer-driven decision making. Their actions honor the human at the end of their decisions, establish a balanced relationship with customers and partners, and put employees in positions to act at work like they'd act at home. Like they were raised.

I grew up Italian, the third of seven kids. We lived a loud and crazy life. But we had a set of behaviors that guided us, which we learned by watching our parents. Their actions, more than words, showed us the path to follow. And their character was on display in how they acted.

The women in my life were particularly animated. My mom, Lydia, would sew until all hours of the night, fashioning custom-made Halloween costumes for each of us, and teeny tiny Barbie doll dresses for my sisters and me. My dad's mom, Ermalinda, rarely sat down for a meal she had prepared. Hovering around the perimeter of the table, she would carry large plates of food, spooning it onto our plates whether we wanted it or not, exclaiming *"Mangia! Mangia!"* ("Eat! Eat!").

And my mom's mom, Virginia, would roll out dough every Christmas to make homemade ravioli. Never satisfied unless they were perfect for us, she would throw out mounds of dough she had rolled out but deemed imperfect, even when it meant putting in hours to begin again. Neither grandma let us leave their homes without handing each of us a bag of groceries, scooping whatever food they had in their pantry for us to take home. They were selfless. They were nourishing. They were perfectionists. They thought of us first.

These are the behaviors that have become the standard for me, and for most of us, for how to act in our lives. We strive to **apply the lessons we learned as kids** to the way we behave at work. As both employees and customers, we gravitate to companies that create environments to

encourage and celebrate these behaviors. These are the make-mom-proud companies we celebrate and learn from in this little book.

As we learn about their paths, it's important to note that each of the make-mom-proud companies did not achieve this state overnight. It took one action, then another, and then another to give people permission and examples to model. That's why, in this book, we offer a simple way to help prompt these actions: a **lens to guide your company decisions,** by thinking of one person in particular at the end of each of them—your mom.

Imagine Mom as your customer.

Within this book, I'm ever so gently delivering a bit of tough love wrapped in velvet to ask you to think about what you do and how you do it—from the perspective of your mother.

I encourage you to ask yourself when you act, speak, respond, or decide, "What would Mom have to say about this?" "Would we do this thing we are contemplating, to her?"

So take a minute. Picture your mom. What's she doing? Picture her picking up the phone to call an 800 number. Then picture her waiting. Picture the frustration of the wait and then her joy as someone connects. And then picture her face as she's asked to repeat all the numbers and facts that she punched in before waiting on hold. Picture her life at the auto dealership. Or walking into a retail store. Picture her nervously waiting for a doctor's appointment. Picture her trying to figure out how to program her phone.

Of course, it's not that simple. It's not the asking of the question "Would we do that to our mother?" that elevates behavior and companies. Conditions must be right for the asking. Leaders must encourage and establish a safe environment where asking that question is celebrated and rewarded. People must be encouraged and enabled to act—by imagining someone they love at the end of decisions.

When asking this question is genuinely enabled, it can benefit every part of your organization. For individuals on the front line, this "Mom lens" can help recalibrate personal responses with customers. Inside the organization and with teams, it prompts collaboration to improve experiences. For leaders, it can be a litmus test to determine actions that the company will, or will not, take to grow.

We need to take how we are treating customers personally. This is what prompts actions that elevate a company and its people. Thinking of our moms at the end of our decisions helps to get us there. That's why I suggest that you imagine her in moments when you're making decisions or taking personal actions. The image of her, of what she's meant to you and what you've learned from her, can be a powerful and instant reality check. It can make us pause.

What imagining Mom, and this book, will do for you.

This book is assembled for you to use inside of your company to get traction on the things that impact and matter in relationships with customers and employees. It is packaged to help you advance your work to "Make Mom Proud." Each of the case studies is organized as a unit for your use inside your organization. You can use them as daily huddles in meetings with leaders or as the content for workshops where you dig deeper.

Each of the four main chapters captures a different aspect of our customer experiences. "Be the Person I Raised You to Be" (chapter 2) addresses the employee experience and the opportunity to elevate and inspire employees' work. "Don't Make Me Feed You Soap!" (chapter 3) concentrates on common issues that define each of our lives as customers and celebrates companies that simplify or extinguish them. "Put Others Before Yourself" (chapter 4) showcases the imperative to redefine what companies offer and how they deliver, starting with customer goals and how they live their lives. "Take the High Road" (chapter 5) celebrates the character and values that live within make-mom-proud companies, and how they overturn or resist traditional business practices to earn goodness-driven growth.

You'll learn actions these companies take to improve, of course. But most important, you'll learn "how" they were able to get traction. I'll share the "inside of their clock" to showcase their decisions and actions and to provide you with decisions you can make to earn the right to growth by improving employee and customer lives. Prodding questions after each case study ask you to look at your company through the "Mom lens" so that you can assess where you are now.

The thirty-two case studies provide you with a mini tool kit to use inside your organization. Each is built with lessons that are easily consumable, broken into individual learning modules, and immediately available to you. Chapter 6, "Stop the Shenanigans!," summarizes all of the "Mom lens" challenges as a quiz or assessment, to determine where you are today on your journey.

I encourage you to join our movement to market hope to customers and encouragement to each other, that improving customer experiences is achievable, and that progress is being made. A dedicated website (http://www.make-mom-proud) is now live, where you can honor your mom and be recognized for your progress. Post a picture of your mom and a summary of what you've done to improve customer and employee experiences (more about this later), so that we can learn your advances. We will use the hashtag **#MakeMomProud** on social media to broadcast your efforts.

This is a celebration book *and* a "tell it like it is" book, because we need both. There are many, many companies that are overturning and redesigning "frustrated mom moments" to create "Make Mom Proud" moments all around the world. In the thirty-two case studies, and numerous anecdotes throughout this book, we celebrate actions that companies have taken to move from "everyday" behavior to acts that elevate a company and its people.

In addition to celebrating these great moments, I'll be "noodging" you, as my Italian grandmas would say, to make change where warranted. As friends, we'll look at some moments where we know we can do better: those "you can't make this stuff up" times in customers'

"I'VE HAD BREAKFAST, LUNCH AND A SNACK. I'VE GAINED
15 POUNDS AND THE CABLE GUY IS STILL NOT HERE."

lives when we make it hard on them, though not intentionally. The plain fact of the matter is that sometimes our lives as customers are not as easy as they're cracked up to be.

To describe these peccadilloes in our businesses, I've turned to humor as shorthand to convey those moments—again, as a friend and as someone living this stuff the same as you are. The custom-created comics smattered across these pages in one brief snippet are intended to capture the customer perspective. And I'll be offering them to you as teaching tools you can access on my website customerbliss.com if you find, as I do, that humor can be both a salve and a catalyst for recognizing an opportunity and driving change.

**Use this book to tell the story of your customers'
lives. Then take actions to "Make Mom Proud."**

This book leads us back to those memories of our childhood, of how we were reared, to simplify how we make decisions in business. It's the simplicity of those childhood lessons that made them easy to follow.

Below is a summary of the chapters of the book, organized to help you cut through the clutter and focus decision making and actions on what matters most so that you can inspire new behaviors inside your company. And grow your business by improving customers' lives.

Chapter 2: "Be the Person I Raised You to Be."

The make-mom-proud companies find the people whose upbringing and values align with what they want their company to stand for. And then they enable them to bring the best version of themselves to work. Selecting who will, and will not, become members of these companies is job number one. But after that, the focus is to help them to prosper. To enable them to achieve, and be true to how they were raised. They nurture memory creators who take joy in their work. And enable people to thrive.

Chapter 3: "Don't Make Me Feed You Soap!"

The make-mom-proud companies are steadfast in removing "bar of soap" moments from customers' lives. These are the moments that make it hard to be a customer: waiting, complexity, uncertainty, and sometimes fear and concern. These companies work to show up more humanely where customers have to put in an inordinate amount of time and effort to get what they need. They turn these moments of struggle into ones of reliability, respect, and caring.

Chapter 4: "Put Others Before Yourself."

The Make-mom-proud companies prove with their actions that they have their customers' best interest in mind. This is at the heart of companies that grow most organically, earning ardent admirers. Operating at this level remains elusive until the paradoxical realization kicks in, which is that to achieve your goals, you need to help others achieve theirs.

To take this approach to growth means opening up everyone to a new order of design and decision making. It goes well beyond "whack-a-moling" problems away to imagining people and emotions and their lives. This starting point enables make-mom-proud companies to design moments that elevate their place in customers' lives.

Chapter 5: "Take the High Road."

Make-mom-proud companies overturn or resist one-sided business practices. They take the road less traveled to earn honor-bound relationships with customers, partners, and employees. They choose to reverse the trend of business practices that have defined their industries.

They establish *balanced* relationships where both sides win, where both customer and company are better off because they are in each other's lives. They honor customers as assets. They work to flip "Gotcha!" moments to "We've got your back" moments. They applaud accountability. They practice reciprocal trust. Their goal is for customers to prosper.

Six Actions That Build Make-Mom-Proud Companies.

Throughout this book, you will be receiving what I found to be a constant source of joy: learning about actions, often bravely undertaken, that elevate companies, and forge genuine and caring bonds between employees, customers, and companies. After studying hundreds of these forward-thinking organizations and leaders, I've distilled their impact down to six most common among them in advancing their practices and operations. In this book, you'll learn about many companies whose actions changed the course of an entire industry. Then you'll learn about others whose strikingly simple actions had lasting impact on their culture and business.

One Action Can Open the Door.

The power of make-mom-proud actions is that, once put into place, they set others in motion. They give people permission to do the right thing. As you'll see in the case studies, any one of these simple actions can start a groundswell for good. For example, in the chapter "Be the Person I Raised You to Be," you'll learn about Cleveland Clinic's transformation. It began with the commitment, accompanied by an investment in training and communication, that everyone in the organization was considered and given permission to act as a "caregiver." Years of actions later, which built upon that commitment, they are rated the number two hospital in the United States by *U.S. News & World Report*.

Actions for Hiring and Development Set the Tone.

You will see the deliberate and well-orchestrated actions that make-mom-proud companies take to hire people whose values and behaviors are in sync with their own. Pal's Sudden Service, a drive-through restaurant based in Tennessee with twenty-six locations, enlists a 60-point psychometric survey to determine whether the teenagers who will deliver food to your drive-in window or make your burger will sync with the values of the company and the team they will join. They then receive more than 120 hours of training and ongoing mentoring. Their turnover is one-third the industry average, and they have lost just seven general managers in thirty-three years. Pal's enjoys one of the highest revenues per square foot in the quick-serve restaurant industry. CEO Thom Crosby connects this to the company's teams, and how they are hired and developed.

Human and Mindful Actions Create Joy.

The make-mom-proud companies provide opportunities that enable their people to take spirited actions, and to be authentic in their gestures and behavior. First Direct Bank took the action to have a human available every day, 24/7. And the humans you reach have your back, and permission to do what's right for you. Every person whom customers reach is trusted to change processes, procedures, and policies to improve their situation. Ninety-two percent of First Direct customers say that they would recommend the bank to someone else.

Acts of Trust Are Necessary.

Lemonade Insurance puts trust first in the manner in which they fulfill member claims. On the Lemonade app, members chat with Lemonade's bot, AI Jim, who asks about what caused their claim. Next, "he" asks them to sign the honesty pledge on the app—a vow made not only to Lemonade, but also to the other members who benefit from fairness in reporting, claims, and payments. Finally, this oh-so-smart and mom-like company, via the person of AI Jim, asks customers to look him in the eye and record a video oath with the reason for the claim. On Lemonade's transparency blog, where it freely shares its performance, it was noted that Lemonade has captured 27 percent of policyholders who are newcomers to insurance in their current New York market area. There is power in the attraction of truth and trust.

Clarity of Purpose Actions Show the Way.

REI generated an estimated 6.7 billion media impressions as it fearlessly closed its doors to encourage everyone to #OptOutside on Black

Friday. Starting with the simple question "How do we want to show up during the holidays?" REI's purpose inspired customers with this action heralded the world over. More than seven hundred companies banded together in REI's movement, and hundreds of state parks offered incentives to get people moving and outside on Black Friday. Financially, REI continues to grow, while its comparable competitors are struggling. Like REI, research proves that organizations who lead with clarity of purpose and deliver on that purpose can outperform the market by more than 350 percent.

Acts of Fairness Earn Word of Mouth and Growth.

Virgin Hotels decided to act with fairness by eliminating "nickel and diming" at their hotels. There is no charge for Wi-Fi. "Bandwidth is a right, not a revenue stream," Virgin communicates to its customers. You also won't get dinged for room service fees or add-on service charges. And there are no fees for early or late check-in. What's getting them the most word of mouth and buzz is their "street pricing" on minibar items. They charge you in the room what you'd pay at the corner market.

"We shouldn't feel like 'we've got you,'" says CEO Raul Leal in rebuffing fees customers often feel imprisoned by at other hotels. After only its first year of business, the Virgin hotel in Chicago was named the number one hotel in the United States by the Condé Nast Traveler Readers' Choice Awards.

"High Road" Actions Earn Love, Admiration, and Advocacy.

The Columbus Metropolitan Library took the action to get rid of late fees. Its objective is to help kids meet their summer reading goal, not worry about that ten-cents-a-day fee. The first major urban library in the United States to do this, its action focuses the organization back to its mission. There is a bit of tracking: you're asked to get that book back in 28 days, which is reasonable. Automatic renewal has been put in place so that instead of calling your book late, it is renewed back to you. Because of this act and many others, the Columbus Metropolitan Library is one of the most progressive and acclaimed libraries in the United States.

In our lives, we remember the companies, the people, and the times when we were honored as a friend, as a partner, as a customer. Two-way trust, open and honest communication, and fearless sharing are cornerstones of the relationships that come to mean the most to us.

And these feelings hold just as true in both our personal and business relationships. These foundational behaviors we learned as kids stay with us all of our lives. Perhaps that's why they are so important as we evaluate the companies and people we want to stay in contact with and do business with.

Picture your mom.

You've pictured your mom. Now, as we close this chapter, picture your life as a customer.

Then picture your customers as they seek support, value, and the delivery of your promise. Picture their lives as your customer, and what they think about in those moments. And how they feel.

Picture your mom's face. Or picture your friend's mom's face. Picture her life. And decide what impact *you* will have on it. As *you* serve your customers. As *you* affect their lives while *you* process their paperwork or fill an order. As *you* make leadership decisions.

Now, ask yourself. Do you ever have to take an action or approve an action or drive your company to take actions that you'd never, ever do to your mom?

Picture Mom as you make decisions and see what happens differently in your business, in your interactions, and in your life. Because at the end of the day, your decisions are what affect customer experiences. They drive customers to either stay with you, or leave you.

Our collective decisions tell each customer a story about who we are, what we value, and about the role we choose to play in their lives. How we choose to correct something that goes wrong—how steadfast we are in delivering the goods, ensuring quality, and keeping our promises—tells customers about how much we think of them on the end of our decisions. And that's what shows up on the internet. That's what grows or gets in the way of our business growth.

You hold the power to improve customers' lives. To make a choice when you act, when you decide, when you choose to react or respond. Simply pause and think: Would I do that to my mother? Then examine and guide your behavior with these four essential business lessons.

2.

Be the Person I Raised You to Be.

*"All I am I owe to my mother.
I attribute all my success in life to the moral, intellectual,
and physical education I received from her."*
–GEORGE WASHINGTON

A little while after Indra Nooyi was named the CEO of PepsiCo, she traveled home to India to visit her mother. The morning after she arrived, piles of visitors began pouring into her mother's home. They walked past Nooyi and straight to her mom, where they congratulated her on her daughter's accomplishment. They praised her for her ability to raise a daughter who would become a CEO. This, Nooyi reflected, made sense. Her mother and late father's guidance was responsible for so much of who she would become, and of her success.

As a result of that experience, Nooyi decided that all of the mothers and fathers of *her* executives deserved the same praise. "It occurred to me that I had never thanked the parents of my executives for the gift of their child to PepsiCo," she recounted in an interview. So after that trip, Nooyi initiated a practice that she continues today.

She personally writes letters to the parents of her top four hundred executives, describing how the values they instilled benefit PepsiCo, saying in them, **"Thank you for the gift of your child to our company."**

The power of what Indra Nooyi does, and the power of all of the make-mom-proud companies, is that they find people whose upbringing and values align with what they want their company to stand for. And then they enable them to bring that version of themselves to work. For Nooyi, those letters of thanks come naturally—a result of hiring leaders who share company values.

Selecting who will, and will not, become members of these companies is job number one. Wegmans, the beloved grocery store on the eastern seaboard of the United States, actually slows down its growth to enable it to find people who fit its core values. The Container Store, a mainstay on *Fortune*'s annual ranking of the 100 best companies to work for, hires only 3 percent of all employees who apply.

But after that, the focus is to help them to prosper. To enable them to achieve, and be true to how they were raised. "We want our employees to be the same person at work as they are at home," the president emeritus of Southwest Airlines, Colleen Barrett, repeatedly says. Isadore Sharp, the founder and CEO of Four Seasons Hotels and Resorts, comments that "It is our work to give people a sense of purpose and the courage to believe in themselves." These companies enable people to bring the best version of themselves to work. That is what we will share and celebrate in this chapter: practices that make-mom-proud companies take to their people and organizations.

Showing Our Humanity at Work.

Our humanity, our *humanness*, more than ever needs to show through in how we do business with customers and each other. And an app alone will not solve everything. With the stratospheric increase in high-tech solutions to "take care" of customers, the need for high touch has also escalated. Customers need a healthy dose of both.

Yes, an app can let you know the arrival time of your repairman, but it is the man and his handshake and how he cares for your home as he walks in that show the kind of mother he has. Yes, you can book your ticket online, but it's the gate agent's concern in making your connection that shows if she's been honored—so she can honor you. Yes, you can pick up your rental car without even talking to a human, but a smile from that guy or gal checking you out can improve the experience. And give you comfort when they're given the authority to let it slide when your return is a few minutes late. High tech without a human connection may make interactions more efficient, but it's important to know when to **blend humanity and caring** into customer experiences.

In her wonderful blog, Michelle Chaffee, a tech founder and health-care professional, writes about her experience with ovarian cancer at what appeared to be cool and high-tech in the beginning:

> *The minute I walked into the new digs of the clinic, I knew it was very different and could get the gist of what they were trying to do. It felt very space age, very Jetsons. Patients were greeted Apple style, by mostly young concierge types standing around at the ready with devices in hand to check you in. This seemed fine and I was intrigued and certainly willing to continue with the adventure.*

But Michelle's experience ended with the ultimate decision to depart after she had been guided by device-carrying concierges for hours, sending her to and fro within that sterile building:

I wanted to scream, "Will someone help me? I'm afraid my can-
cer has spread!" But, by this point I knew it wouldn't make any
difference. . . . As I headed out the door, I unclipped the GPS
tracking device from my shirt and dropped it in the designated
receptacle. No, I did not make that up for effect. They really did
give me a GPS device so they could "find me" when it was time
for my appointment.

Michelle's experience shows that more tech alone cannot always
assuage customer fear, worry, or concern.

What will unfold for you in this chapter are behaviors that **enable
employees to thrive**. Eight case studies showcase leadership and
company practices that build prosperity of the human spirit and earn
financial prosperity. They put people into a position to succeed by
mentoring and guiding them to outcomes they are proud to deliver,
remove barriers to delivering value, and trust people with the authority to make good decisions. They give them the tools and ability to
guide and take care of all customers they might encounter, and trust
them with the relationships that are in their hands.

These are behaviors that find a comfortable home inside the companies that "Make Mom Proud." They make hiring the most important decision, and then encourage and enable people to bring the best
version of themselves to work.

Honor the Dignity of Customers' Lives.

Simply, enable people to care.

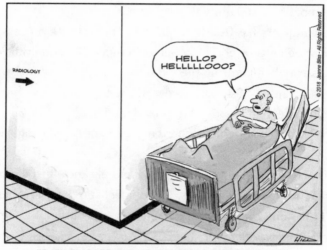

"THEY PRICKED ME WITH NEEDLES, MOVED ME TO
A HALLWAY AFTER A SCAN...AND FORGOT ME."

You matter. From time to time as a customer, you might feel that you don't. Me too. That's what happened to Michelle Chaffee. As efficient as the processes she went through were meant to be, they inadvertently designed the heart out of them. The "concierge" Michelle encountered behaved more like a people mover and process handler than a care provider. Sometimes "process" doesn't include taking care of the human inside of it. And that can happen in a variety of industries.

Would you roll your mother into a hospital hallway and then leave her there? Of course not. But this type of thing sometimes happens because someone has a specific task to execute and he or she does it. Probably correctly. But even with each person executing her task perfectly, your mom may still end up alone on that gurney in the hallway. One person takes her from her room to wait for her test and leaves her there. Another does the test, then moves her back to the hallway to wait for someone to pick her up. And there she waits. That's because processes established for their efficiency might not factor your mom's emotions and dignity into the equation.

Every industry has frontline employees tasked with processing patients, taking calls or checking out customers. But sometimes when the focus is only on getting the job done, caring for the human at the center of it can get lost. Employees are not mere people movers or process handlers—they are *care* providers. Every part of the organization is either caring directly for customers or supporting someone who is.

This is our grand opportunity to let people know that they matter. Treating customers with dignity and respect starts with treating employees the same way. In order to deliver customer dignity, employees need to feel it, experience it, and receive it themselves. And they need to be encouraged to weave the delivery of dignity into their interactions with customers. Simply, enable people to care.

The make-mom-proud companies build a company of people who take *care* of customers and their lives. They unite employees in delivering so that no matter what part of the company customers encounter, caring is consistent. They ensure "one company" continuity of care.

Caring for Those Who Care.

They also take care of those who *do* the caring. Sometimes the barrier to human connection with customers is composed of employees who need a boost. Every person who lives his life on the front line at one point or another needs a little empathy extended his way. He needs a pep talk, a hug, or a reprieve. Emotionally he is spent, or he is intellectually exhausted from putting customers back to a state of peace of mind.

In healthcare, when the emotional toil gets high, many hospitals practice a support system called "Code Lavender." Initially established in a hospital in Hawaii to give emotional support to patients and family members suffering through life-altering moments, its practice has been extended to care for those who care. Calling Code Lavender brings to caregivers needed urgent emotional sustenance to help them overcome highly emotional and draining situations. Core to its success is making it safe for caregivers to call the code—with no judgment or worry. These caring time-outs help people to rebalance so that they can continue with their important work. How do you care for those who give care in your company?

When "care" is foundational to how you show up as a company, human needs prompt innovation. It overcomes organizational boundaries. It sets companies and its people apart. All employees need to be enabled to care. And they need to be encouraged to link arms, to weave the delivery of care and dignity across all of their interactions with customers.

Here's how Cleveland Clinic embedded "caring" into its entire organization. It makes sure that your mom is never sitting alone on a gurney in a hallway or in her hospital room waiting for help. Most important, this practice lifts up everyone to the role of "caregiver," connecting the entire organization to its pursuit of improving lives with dignity. As you read Cleveland Clinic's story, think of what your version of the "no pass zone" is. How do you unite your entire organization to care about the lives of customers, and one another? **Do you show up as a company that cares?**

Cleveland Clinic Made EVERY Employee a "Caregiver"

DECISION INTENT: Engage all employees in honoring the dignity of patients. Cleveland Clinic, a multispecialty academic hospital in Cleveland, Ohio, lives by a guiding principle: "Patients First." They wanted guiding action, not words to hold everyone accountable for patient and family care. Realizing the burden of care that patients and family members have to grapple with in other aspects of their health-care experience, Cleveland Clinic wants to ensure that in *its* house, everyone is united in caring for patients' emotional, physical, and educational needs and desires.

ACTION TO #MAKEMOMPROUD: First they began a simple "No Pass Zone." This rule leaves no room for interpretation: if you're near a patient's room and see that the call light is on, no matter what your job is, you go in to see how you can help. Don't let a patient wait. Take care of the life. Honor the dignity.

But no single rule will stick without the foundational actions and commitment to ensure its success. Cleveland Clinic invests in training more than fifty-one thousand employee caregivers on the emotional and experience of care. **They also fuse together everyone's work by giving all employees the title of CAREGIVER**. Previously reserved for physicians only (all others were called nonprofessional staff), everyone including therapists, janitors, nurses, groundskeepers, and receptionists all bear the responsibility to care for patient's lives. The person cleaning a room, saying hello and fluffing a pillow, can affect someone's day with her kindness, just as much as a physician, nurse, or therapist administering medical assistance.

Finally, **they follow multidiscipline team rounding of patients** to care for the "whole patient"—which they call *Managing the 360*. This process assigns multidiscipline teams of employees to cover each shift, so that patients do not have to knit together their own healthcare. Patients and families have the confidence of knowing teams are united and working together on their behalf.

EVERYONE at Cleveland Clinic Has the Title Caregiver. #MakeMomProud.

IMPACT: *"Patients come to us for high quality care—but they don't like us very much,"* Dr. Delos "Toby" Cosgrove said in 2010, when he became CEO and initiated the caring movement. Now they earn accolades as one of the most patient-centered healthcare providers. Cleveland Clinic consistently achieves a "recommend" rating of more than 80 percent, well in the 90th percentile of all hospitals measured via the HCAHPS (Hospital Consumer Assessment of Healthcare Providers and Systems) national health-care measure. As an overall hospital system, *U.S. News & World Report* ranks Cleveland Clinic as the number two hospital in the United States.

THE MOM LENS

Intuitive, genuine, and proactive people #MakeMomProud.

Cleveland Clinic elevates everyone in their organization to "Caregiver," giving all staff the tools, the authority, and the honor to work together to give patients and families comfort. They unite to care for both the emotional and physical needs of each patient.

Do You Show Up as a "Caring" Company?

Is Everyone United to Care for Customers, Regardless of Role?

Trust the Front Line to Extend Grace.

Let policy and the Golden Rule collide.

"I FEEL AWFUL THAT YOU'RE JUST 3 DAYS OUT OF WARRANTY. IF I HAD A DELOREAN, YOU COULD GO BACK FOR THE EXTENDED WARRANTY."

Would you turn down your mom's warranty claim three days out of warranty? No—you would want to hear her story. You'd want to know her customer history. And if you're on the front line, you'd want to be given the chance to make an informed decision. You'd want the company to honor your decision because you had gathered more facts to guide its outcome than could be covered by a blanket policy. You'd want your decision honored based on the values, empathy, and ability you were hired for.

When we are validated, and even the slightest concession is made to accommodate us as customers, it makes a difference. And that difference contributes to how we stack up the companies we will go back to and talk about.

This is not a plea to throw company profits out the door by loosening every rule willy-nilly. It's about preparing employees. It's about enabling employees to act in situations where valued customers are at risk. It's about letting them make the call to let a few hours slide off a car rental return because they have a high-value customer in front of them. Or honoring that warranty claim for your mom three days out of warranty, because it's the right thing to do.

Let Policy and the Golden Rule Collide.

As we become increasingly self-sufficient in almost every part of our lives as customers, it becomes even more urgent that when someone connects with the humans of your company, the contact is meaningful. The authenticity of those connections, people's ability to *really* help, and the front line's respect for the customer—because they themselves are respected—are now more critical than ever. "Doing" human interactions well in an increasingly self-service world will set you apart.

Companies that are putting in the work to enable this change are reaping the rewards. Mercedes Benz USA, for example, began taking this approach in their Customer Assistance Centers, enabling call center reps to balance standard operating procedure with information about the customers they assist. In many cases, the informed exceptions they make lead to increased advocacy and a more profitable customer.

A study of twenty thousand customers by C Space measuring the CQ, or Customer Quotient, validates the importance of outreach that is worth customers' time and honors their needs—especially when they choose to stray from the self-service path. Customers want openness, relevance, empathy, experience, and emotion. These are all experiences frontline folks want to deliver, but they need permission and the ability to extend grace.

What we know, and you know as a customer, is that most of us don't make it our intention to "take" a company for anything. We want to be treated fairly. We want to be known. We want to be honored when, inevitably, Murphy's law kicks in and that warranty expires the day before our computer wipes out its motherboard or the brakes go skittish on our car or that vacuum cleaner we just bought goes on the fritz.

Often at these times we encounter someone who sheepishly has to tell us the bad news. And stand by whatever limits their ability to help, even though it makes them squeamish. And that news is "Sorry, I can't do anything for you."

But what if the front line was trusted with some wiggle room to make a judgment to do the right thing for the customer before them? What if they were prepared to act in these moments?

Easier said than done. Moving from talk to action here requires knowing which "You're kidding!" customer experiences should be planned ahead of time to give employees wiggle room. It requires giving employees customer information so they know the value of the person needing the exception, and training and support for its delivery. And most important, **trust, to let good people think on their feet and make the right call.** Here's a story that illustrates this. When John bought his laptop, he also purchased the extended warranty and damage coverage. Having had some expensive issues with his previous laptop, he wanted to make sure he was covered. Exactly three days after his warranty ran out he opened his laptop to white horizontal lines running vertically down the screen (anyone who's ever seen this display *knows* John's pain). He had spent more than $300 for the warranty, and within its coverage period he had used it only for one minor incident right after he purchased the computer. John felt that the company would cover him, and brought the computer in to be taken care of. He was immediately told that his warranty had expired, and offered him computer replacement options.

Undeterred, he asked to speak to a supervisor, who reminded John that he'd known the warranty when he purchased it, and those were the terms. "Three days, only three days!" John exclaimed. They said there was nothing they would do for him.

The make-mom-proud companies prepare the front line to make sound judgment calls with customers. With data, knowledge, training, and trust, they enable them to make smart decisions in these moments. They honor the front line by honoring their ability to make informed decisions to keep valued customers. Do you guide and offer trusting guidelines to enable people to extend grace?

This next case study is about the cultural belief system that guides Oberoi Hotels in whom they hire, how they develop all who work there, and how the common belief system that all who work there share to guide their collective behavior. At Oberoi Hotels, considered some of the finest and most exclusive in the world, you will be intrigued to learn about what they do to give employees the confidence and tools to make good decisions, resulting in customer growth, marketplace stature, and customer advocacy.

A Case Study to #MakeMomProud

The Oberoi Group Decided... to Let Employees Decide

DECISION INTENT: Enable employees to choose the right response. When guests enter any one of India's Oberoi Group properties, considered some of the most exclusive in the world, expectations are high the minute they make their reservation. Guests expect not only to be served, but to be treated as guests: they want their *needs* anticipated. And when a situation arises of any sort, they expect action, not process.

ACTION TO #MAKEMOMPROUD: Train in emotional intelligence & trust. The Oberoi Group focuses its energy on hiring people with the values and attributes consistent with the standards of their *Dharma*—the Oberoi code of ethics. Once someone is onboard, she is trusted and held responsible for upholding those attributes in her personal behavior and in how she treats guests and fellow employees. To enable employees to understand and read each situation correctly, Oberoi invests in emotional intelligence training. It chooses not to have the front line guided by a manual or a set of rules, but instead, it invests in guiding and coaching in the training that leads to the right response for the right guest. Rather than setting up their employees with a set of policies to follow, they educate them in building the skill set so *they* can decide the right response. Employees are able to create meaningful interactions: they will not settle for letting their customers "get by."

Fear that the front line will "give away the store" can be a reason for overruling instead of trusting employees to give the correct, proportionate response. However, companies that train and enable employees to read the situation find that the freedom they give is rarely abused. For example, it's well known that Ritz-Carlton gives employees up to $2,000 to spend per day if they need to. Most don't get anywhere near that—but they are honored to be trusted. Oberoi found that too. Trust given is a privilege that employees rise to, making employees want to stay and customers more connected to them.

The Oberoi Group Trains in Emotional Intelligence. #MakeMomProud.

IMPACT: The Oberoi Group is ranked eighth in India's best places to work. A recent process that Oberoi gave to its employees to extend grace proves the effectiveness of enabling and trusting employees. Guest Net Promoter Scores rose to 86 from 81 previously—a very difficult level to achieve once a company has achieved a level of customer advocacy in the 80s. Employees entrusted with extending that grace honored the privilege, using it as if it were their own to give. Those who are trusted give trust in return.

THE MOM LENS

Trusting and holding people accountable to take the right action #MakesMomProud.

Oberoi Hotels and Resorts hires people whose values align with their code of ethics. And then they guide, trust, and enable them to make the right call to honor, extend grace, and grow their customers.

Do You Trust the Front Line to Extend Grace?

Can You Let Policy and the Golden Rule Collide?

Hire People with the Ability to Care.

Make hiring your most important decision.

Stopping to get a tank of gas and a snack may not seem like an experience to obsess about. But at QuikTrip, it *is* their obsession. QuikTrip hires people with the ability to care—selecting only about one out of every one hundred applicants. They teach rigorous use of daily checklists to ensure that the coffee and food are fresh and the bathrooms are clean. And QuikTrip people are coached on personalizing both service and *care.* So when you walk in dragging three tired kids behind you, a QuikTrip hire will give you a hand with the door and treat you all to ice cream. Because you look like you could use one.

Would you tell your mom you couldn't help her without first empathizing with her, and trying to find a solution? QuikTrip and the make-mom-proud companies work to ensure that won't happen when you interact with them, because they focus on filling up their companies with people who care. They make hiring their most important decision.

As we move past many of the traditional ways of interacting with companies, what we expect from the people across the chat box, sales counter, or service desk has changed dramatically. The newest breed of customer especially is choosing to interact with companies that provide caring, relevance, choice, and speed. The ability to empathize and "be human" is now cited as a reason customers stay or go. It is their condition for keeping the relationship and earning the sale. All customers are not *always* right, but all deserve to be cared for with dignity and respect.

This plays for all of us though, doesn't it? Social media feedback from every type of customer group cites how much company employees understood who they were, or if they "got them." These are deciding factors for engaging deeper with a company or weaning from it: making how you hire and whom you hire an increasing priority for business growth.

Make Hiring Your Most Important Decision.

Niki Leondakis, CEO of Equinox Fitness Clubs, recounted her story at a conference of a hotel experience you may have also had. After an early run one morning, she got back to her hotel, dying for a cup of coffee. The restaurant wasn't open yet, so Leondakis asked the front desk clerk if she would grab a cup of coffee from the kitchen for her.

What the front desk clerk told her was that the restaurant would be open in ten minutes. She couldn't help her, but why not? That hotel clerk could easily have walked a few steps into the kitchen, where the coffee was surely brewing by then, to get Ms. Leondakis a cup of coffee. A small act of kindness that would have earned gratitude and a customer singing her praises. Instead, her behavior was cited by Le-ondakis at a conference, in this book, and likely across a lot of social media.

In these moments when your customer is in need, or has a worry or problem, people chosen for their ability to care rise to the occasion. In fact, *failure to empathize* or take the customers' situation seriously is one of the most cited reasons for customers to walk away from a company and its people.

Hiring people with the ability to care will fuel your growth. Make-mom-proud companies take the time to make the interview go beyond questions involving just aptitude and skill; they get to know the human behind the résumé. They learn about the person whose actions will define who they are as people to customers, partners, and the marketplace.

Here is one of my favorite stories about a company that takes the time to really know about the people who might join their team. They learn whether they jibe culturally and probe for people who demonstrate "light behind their eyes" and empathy in who they are as people.

You wouldn't imagine that a fast-food drive-through would be so deliberate about how they hire that they actually screen for attitude and aptitude, but Pal's Sudden Service does. They take great pains to make sure you feel you're getting cared for as you're ordering your burger and fries! How does your company understand who belongs in your culture and interacting with customers?

A Case Study to #MakeMomProud

Pal's Sudden Service Decided They Would Screen and Hire for Character

DECISION INTENT: Find happy and content teenagers. With more than 90 percent of their thousand-person workforce part time and 40 percent of them sixteen-to-eighteen-year-olds, Pal's wanted to ensure that they could spot people of great character to represent who they are and be part of their team. And all at lightning speed! They have just eighteen seconds at the drive-up window and twelve seconds at the food delivery window to connect with customers as human and caring. This is Pal's secret sauce: instead of focusing the least on their entry-level employees, they focus on them the most.

ACTION TO #MAKEMOMPROUD: Screen for attitude and attributes we learned as kids. Pal's went to school on how to hire by studying their own folks who were thriving. They turned those behaviors and character observations into a 60-point, psychometric survey to decide if employee candidates are a fit for Pal's. Not your run-of-the-mill application, Pal's asks a few mom-approved questions candidates have to agree or disagree with:

- "For the most part, I am happy with myself."
- "I think it is best to trust people you have just met."
- "Raising your voice may be one way to get someone to accept your point of view."

"We're believers that birds of a feather flock together," said CEO Thomas A. Crosby, speaking to the Harvard Business Review. "If you start having an operation with weak crew training and not a lot of really good leadership by managers, the people who apply there are the same kinds of people. We go the opposite direction." Once employees are hired, they receive 120 hours of training before they can work independently without their coach. And Pal's, Thom Crosby, and his leadership spend 10 percent of their time daily mentoring team members on a skill or an aptitude. It's a daily commitment that Pal's provides to develop not only great fry cooks, but also great humans. Pal's is so clear about who they will and will not hire that they don't grow at a speed until a manager is ready to lead a store. They won't sacrifice their culture for growth, Crosby says.

Pal's Sudden Service is a Character Coach. #MakeMomProud.

IMPACT: Pal's employee turnover rate is one-third the industry average. They have lost just seven general managers in thirty-three years. Based on their success, Pal's established the Business Excellence Institute, identified as being one of the leaders in food-service training for leadership and management practices. They are the first restaurant chain to win the Malcolm Baldrige National Quality Award, sponsored by the National Institute of Standards and Technology of the U.S. Department of Commerce. *Inc.* magazine named Pal's to its list of 25 Most Audacious Companies. Pal's enjoys one of the highest revenues per square foot in the quick-serve restaurant industry, with store revenue that has increased by about 300 percent since 1995.

THE MOM LENS

Deliberate Hiring to Build a United Culture #MakesMomProud.

Pal's Sudden Service screens for the aptitudes and attitudes we learned as kids in their hiring process, ensuring that only those who fit their culture are invited to a place on the team.

Is Hiring Your Most Important Decision?

How Do You Get to Know the Human Behind the Résumé?

Remove Survey Score Begging.

Improve the life; earn the score.

"YOU'D LIKE ME TO **RATE** MY MAMMOGRAM EXPERIENCE ON A SCALE OF 1 TO 10? IS THAT FOR CUSTOMER SERVICE OR PAIN?"

A long time ago in a galaxy far, far away, surveys began for the pure and simple reason to improve customers' lives. Then, in an effort to motivate performance, people started getting paid for the score. **And then the begging began.**

When did "Would you give me a 10" become part of the language of our lives as customers? Many point to the automotive industry as the beginning of the survey score culture. One of the first verticals to stack rack brands by survey score, auto makers started sending out surveys to car owners asking how dealers did with their car purchase or service experience. They footed the bill for the survey so that they could see the performance of dealers. Then, they attached the achievement of rewards, car allocation, and bonuses based on survey performance.

"Yes . . . We value your opinion, but we want a 10! So please just don't fill out our survey unless you can give us that 10." Around the world that survey score has become the endgame. Would you do that to your mother?

Extending moms' benefit of the doubt here, initiating surveys and attaching results to how people earned bonus and compensation were well intentioned. But something weird happens when people's ability to pay for their kids' braces or put a new roof on their house is based on how high that score is.

Now nearly every type of industry asks customers to complete surveys. Hotels, hospitals, insurance companies, pet stores, airlines—you name it. A friend of mine recently received a survey to rate the experience of her mammogram on a scale of zero to ten. Yikes. **Would you invite your mom to dinner, and then ask her to rate your meal?**

In one of my early Chief Customer Officer (CCO) roles, as I was getting acclimated to the company, I saw huge rolls of gold foil stickers with "GIVE US A 10!" on them. In a very unpopular act at the time, I tossed them all away. It turned out to be the right approach because once we stopped begging for scores, we began to get real and authentic feedback that helped the company improve. When we changed our inquiry from "Tell us why you can't give us a 10" to "Tell us how we can help your life," the purpose of the feedback shifted and we could finally use it to make advances.

The opportunity to improve customers' lives and receive their honest and fearless feedback should be a gift. But we've injected fear into the process by paying for top scores and stack-ranking performers in an attempt to get them to rise to their competitors.

In all of this score chasing, we've missed the opportunity to guide the culture of a company toward the improvement of customers' lives. And it is bugging customers, and turning them away. In fact, "PLEASE GIVE ME TOP SCORES" is the fourth most annoying interaction customers have with companies, according to the Dialog Direct Customer Rage Study.

Improve the life; <u>earn</u> the score.

Instead of starting with the score, I encourage you to start with the story of customers' lives. Find out what's really going better for your customers as you adjust and improve the experiences they're having with their company. What's more, start real conversations within your organization. What stories are they telling about their customers' experiences? Are they paying attention? Seek operational and behavioral performance that both individuals and teams can "earn" that contribute to the score, and compensate them on those actions focused on taking care of customers.

When you can release the front line from the directive of chasing a score, and instead inspire and motivate them to take actions to improve customers' lives, their roles are elevated. Paradoxically, that direction and leadership language and guidance in the long run will improve your scores. (For the right reasons. Not because you begged for them.)

Here is how Safelite AutoGlass elegantly asks customers for feedback, while putting that score in its rightful place. They use it to elevate an understanding of customer needs and priorities, to coach and guide, and to drive company improvement.

A Case Study to #MakeMomProud

Safelite AutoGlass Coaches for Behavior, Not Scores.

DECISION INTENT: Enable the front line to do their best work. The eight thousand associates who interact with customers, taking their calls and repairing or replacing their windshields, are the spirit and face of Safelite. And Tom Feeney, Safelite's CEO, considers them heroes. "The rest of us are here to support them," he told me. At Safelite, frontline employees are provided with an engaging work environment that empowers them to be at their personal best. Leaders engage, coach, and develop their people to enable them to do their best work.

ACTION TO #MAKEMOMPROUD: Guide behaviors that exhibit "the Safelite Spirit" rather than pushing for scores. "Success" for Safelite is prepared employees. They look for people who connect with customers on an emotional level, demonstrating a service mind-set, a can-do attitude, and a caring heart with each other and with their customers. These are the behaviors tied to incentives and recognition programs. To Safelite, metrics are the *outcome* of behaviors. They encourage and trust employees to make decisions based on what's right, to live in the "gray," and to know when to make exceptions and go above and beyond standard procedures. Leaders act to help employees achieve success by providing them with the tools and latitude they need to deliver service so great, it's memorable. Tom told me, "We are not metric-bound, we are mission bound; to enabling and guiding our people to live the Safelite Spirit."

Safelite Guides to Improve Behavior, Not Survey Scores. #MakeMomProud.

IMPACT: Feeney told me that the biggest impact he is seeing is in the behavior of the front line. And in how they are personalizing the work they do and the way that they respond to customers' needs inside and outside the scope of the work order they are completing. Tom relayed the story about a Safelite employee who replaced the window in the pickup truck for a woman whose husband had recently died. She was tight on money, given her situation, and expressed embarrassment about the condition of her property at home. The Sunday following her service, her technician knocked on her door and told her, "With your permission, I'm here to cut your lawn. I just want to help you." "THAT is my proof that this is working!" Tom said. "As we have shifted from being only metric-oriented to guiding and encouraging, we are seeing The Safelite Spirit come to life in these stories. It is inspiring extraordinary acts, and bringing them joy in their work."

THE MOM LENS

Focusing on the Life, and Not That Survey Score, #MakesMomProud!

Safelite AutoGlass focuses on coaching behavior that lifts up both employees and customers so that they earn, but never beg for, good results.

DO YOU FOCUS (A BIT TOO MUCH) ON THAT SURVEY SCORE?

Do You Give Employees Time, Ability, and Guidance to Improve?

Check Your Bias at the Door.

Earn customer respect by respecting them first.

THE WOMAN ASKS, BUT THE MAN GETS ANSWERED.

When Mary walked into the high-end shoe retail store she had been eyeing for months, it was a great moment for her. Two months earlier she had fallen in love with a pair of boots she couldn't afford. Determined to eventually buy them, she put herself on a savings plan until she finally had the cash to purchase them.

But when she walked through the door of that store, yearning to be being fawned over by a salesperson eager to slip her feet into those exquisite shoes, she experienced a surprise. No one approached her. There were plenty of people on the floor, but they were focusing on the women dressed in high-end clothing that matched the price of her coveted shoes.

Undeterred, she asked someone to help find the boots she had come to purchase. She was directed to a display across the room. When she walked across the store again to find someone to bring them to her in her size, a salesperson delivered the shoes and left. Mary noticed everyone else in the store as they were fitted for shoes with great care, and how no one fawned over her.

What happened next surprised Mary: those boots had lost their luster. She realized she desired *the experience* of being a customer in that store as much as those boots. When no one came to check on her, she had had enough. She left without the boots.

Would you size up your mother's age or outfit to determine whether you should serve her? You already know the answer to that question. In any setting, someone who walks through your door can't be sized up by his gender, or by what he wears, or whom he walks in with. When you judge your customer, you lessen your humanity. So, check your bias at the door. Suspend judgment. Invest in relationships without the filter.

You may have had a similar experience in your life as a customer. But it's impossible to tell people's "worth" by how people carry themselves, how they look, or what they sound like on the phone. Most important, every person is worthy of being honored, of being approached, and of being welcomed.

Earn customer respect by respecting them first.

Every customer deserves good service and a little "swooning," which Mary so much looked forward to. In fact, I always walk into high-end retail stores without makeup and in jeans and a simple blouse and sneakers. Neat and tidy, but not dolled up—it's my litmus test for understanding the attitude of the folks on the floor, and how they've been trained to check their bias at the door.

When people are taken care of without bias, when they are really heard and understood and have their needs delivered, that is the beginning of cementing a long-term and potentially high-value relationship. This is simply about respect. And it's about developing inclusive and respectful behaviors.

"Diversity is getting asked to the party, while inclusion is getting asked to dance at the party," explains Heidi Grant-Halvorson, PhD, of the NeuroLeadership Institute. This is our opportunity to ask our employees and customers to dance at the party—by including them and respecting them without bias.

This next story is about ThirdLove, a product development company and retailer that recognized an unconscious bias in the women's apparel industry. Generations of women have experienced unconscious bias by the "nude" tone in certain garments, which only applies to women of a certain skin tone, thereby excluding all the rest. Through awareness and inclusion, ThirdLove has changed that, with an inclusive color palette honoring all skin tones, earning accolades of women everywhere. Does any unconscious bias exist in your business that excludes or inadvertently leaves out a portion of your customers and employees?

A Case Study to #MakeMomProud

ThirdLove Decided to Honor All Women of Color.

DECISION INTENT: Honor women of all colors. ThirdLove cofounder Heidi Zak couldn't find a bra that wasn't a painful fit. From that need, she and her husband, Dave, founded FirstLove, where Zak uses her robust data science skills (acquired as a Google marketer) to understand buying habits and customer sentiment and needs. Through this understanding came an opportunity for inclusiveness about the color nude. Usually a pinkish-beige color—that color is the nude skin tone for only *one* set of women. Zak decided to correct a worldwide lack of inclusiveness for women of color in her product category, by developing a range of bra colors that included every skin tone.

ACTION TO #MAKEMOMPROUD: Develop the "New Nudes." ThirdLove's company mission has been to serve *every woman*. Inclusiveness is at the foundation of product design and business conduct. To achieve this, research in understanding women's needs is thorough and constant. An early study of 2.5 million women globally, for example, gathered 9 million data points about sizing. This led to an expansion of sizing to include forty-seven sizes for women between traditional sizing who had never been served before. Very vocal customer feedback also told Zak that women of color felt excluded by the definition of *nude*. The whole idea of this coloration was that it would blend with the color of the skin against which it was worn and not show up under a white blouse, for example.

In response to this need, FirstLove established the "New Nakeds," a five-color palette in its products to include all women. Following ThirdLove's guiding principle of using data to drive business decisions, focus groups and concentrated data guided this decision and outcome. It took two years of research and development to blend colors for women's real skin tone. With these five, all women of color can find a tone that works for them.

ThirdLove Products Serve All Women of Color. #MakeMomProud.

IMPACT: ThirdLove is a disrupter new to the market. Early indications from the people who back this company as well as its customer advocacy to date cannot be ignored. Founded in 2013, its investors include Laurie Ann Goldman, former CEO of Spanx; Lori Greeley, former CEO of Victoria's Secret stores; John Hamlin, chairman of REI; Barry Sternlicht, founder of Starwood Hotels; and Claire Bennett, former executive vice president at American Express and member of the board of directors of Tumi. ThirdLove grew 400 percent from 2014 to 2015, during its critical period of proof of concept. While women buy new bras every year, ThirdLove customers typically buy a second bra within just forty-five days.

THE MOM LENS

Behaving and Acting as an Inclusive Brand #MakesMomProud.

ThirdLove recognizes every skin color in its product offerings. It earns growth through respectful product design and honoring all women.

Do You Invest in Relationships Without Bias?

Is Growth Earned Through Inclusive and Respectful Behavior?

Stop the "Crazy Rules."

Remove rules that inhibit employees,
diminish their spirit, and may send customers packing.

Would you make your mom live by a rule that made no sense? Of course not. But over time, rules seep into our businesses. And as much as employees work to smooth things over, your customers know them, and feel their impact. They can spot an account manager or phone rep exhausted by them—especially as they make apologies for having to uphold them.

Do you have any rules that inhibit employees' ability to serve and that diminishes their spirit? Rules that customers question? If you do, don't feel too bad. Every company has them, and for some reason they tend to live long lives. What sets the make-mom-proud companies apart is that they are constantly on the lookout for them.

These are often crazy things like not honoring a cancellation if it is made within seven days of the final day of a contract. Or charging a fee to your best customers to redeposit their miles for a canceled trip. Or not opening an account until a piece of paper has been delivered both electronically and by mail.

Why is it so hard for companies to spot crazy rules? Because, as companies, we have a lot of them. It's hard to find all the rules that don't make sense or disrupt customer relationships. But it is our job to both diminish those that impede customer growth and reduce employees' role in having to defend them.

These rules show up in *every* kind of business. To squash out unnecessary rules, Hootsuite has even created a "Czar of Bad Systems." After Hootsuite's approval process to gift a company t-shirt cost the company $200 in time and resources, they took action to kill the crazy rules. That defunct Hootsuite process is a perfect example of rules that made sense once but has since outlived its usefulness.

When these rules negatively impact customers' lives, they impact customers, employees, and the bottom line. Your best customers get increasingly vocal as they run into them repeatedly. And your front line must then try their hand at getting an exception or finding a workaround. Crazy rules prompt customers to play costly "service roulette" (you've done it, right?), tapping company resources by repeatedly contacting the company until they reach someone who can swat away the rule or get the outcome they desire.

This is your opportunity to make it easier on employees to deliver value to customers. Perhaps you might follow the lead of Commerce Bank (now TD Bank) that lifted up the spirits of all employees by simply asking them, "What's getting in your way?" "What stupid rules can we kill?" Leaders worked to squash those that they could. And the company celebrated the folks who identified them as heroes.

Rules that require employees to do workarounds exhaust them because they are constantly trying to make things right. And employees who have to work harder to get their work done to serve customers are less happy at work and more likely to depart. In fact, Maritz research found only 8 percent of employees who believe their company's policies and procedures make it easy to satisfy customers.

This next story gets to the heart of elevating the spirit of an organization by giving more ownership to employees. That's where so many of these rules affect employees over time—their inability to have a say in outcomes with customers. Here's how Vail Resorts' people never show up as "policy cops." Just the opposite, Vail has banned the phrase "Our policy is . . . " from conversations with customers. It gives employees permission instead to be curators of joy.

A Case Study to #MakeMomProud

Vail Resorts Decided to Ban *"Our policy is…"* from Guest Conversations.

DECISION INTENT: Let everyone deliver "the experience of a lifetime." Every day on Vail Mountain in Colorado and at its fifteen other ski resorts the goal of Vail Resorts is to build a culture of joy. And that joy needs to include both customers and employees. Vail doesn't want the front line to have to follow standardized service scripts. Or a big pile of rules for what they can and cannot do.

Far from it, Vail wants their folks to bend any rules they need to in order to deliver that joy. They don't have strict guidelines, for example, on when and how often a ski patrol representative can pick up someone whom they've watched do multiple falls and face plants, and offer the skier a refresher course, at no charge. They tell everyone to "go out there and have fun." They are encouraged to be themselves, and bring *their own version of joy* to guests.

ACTION TO #MAKEMOMPROUD: Let people make their fun your own. Vail employees are encouraged to take ownership for delivering joy, and are encouraged to delete these comments from their vocabulary: "I can't do that, our policy is," "Next," "I don't know," "You'll have to . . . ," and "It's not my job. . . ." The front line has permission to take actions as they see fit—to be purveyors of joy. And they're provided with a pocketful of rule-bending gestures they can extend, such as giving free lift tickets when the lift is stopped more than fifteen minutes, or offering a mom and her kids hot chocolate and burgers because they look famished and freezing. Folks are encouraged to make the experience their own. Vail works to remove the rules and constraints, and give people the power to act.

"Joy reinforcement" continues in daily encouragement, and as on-the-spot "epic" experience pins are passed out. Coaching and reviews focus on the behaviors employees exhibit to make fun happen: being inclusive, welcoming, approachable, and positive.

Vail Resorts lets the front line deliver joy. #MakeMomProud.

IMPACT: Vail Resorts is the world's largest ski resort operator, with more than a hundred thousand brand advocates built through the experiences they deliver on and off the slopes. It is the most expensive, but still the most popular in its industry. Vail has more than thirty thousand employees, and many of those employees cite being able to deliver the "experience of a lifetime" as a top driver for why they stay. For three years running, the National Ski Areas Association has recognized one of Vail's properties, Beaver Creek, with its Best Overall Customer Service Program Award.

THE MOM LENS

Elevating Purpose Over Policy #MakesMomProud.

Vail Resorts earns its place at the top because it nurtures and frees employees to deliver their purpose, trusting them to deliver joy and the "experience of a lifetime."

Do You Have Rules That Inhibit People's Ability to Serve?

What Can You Do to Nurture Frontline Heroes Rather Than Policy Cops?

Reward for
Congruence of Heart and Habit.

Celebrate and reward people for their humanity and spirit.

"YEAH, WE REWARD STUFF LIKE THIS HERE."

Blogger Lauren Casper and her husband, John, had navigated their way through their local Trader Joe's store as best they could. The trip had turned a bit chaotic with the two children, and Lauren described how they were rushing to get done and out of the store. "Not only are we two white parents with a brown son and daughter," she said as she described her day, "but our son has noticeable developmental delays and different behaviors caused by his autism, and our daughter has physical differences with her missing and webbed digits."

She was close to tears from the outing when she heard someone call out to her in the parking lot. A young woman who worked at Trader Joe's, whom Lauren described as resembling her adopted daughter, held out a Trader Joe's bouquet to her. As she delivered it to Lauren, she said, "I was adopted as a baby and it has been a wonderful thing. We need more families like yours."

This type of action is not uncommon for Trader Joe's employees, who are hired and rewarded for team collaboration, innovation, and taking the initiative to delight customers, as Lauren Casper experienced with her family. From always walking a customer (never pointing) to that can of garbanzo beans you can't find to the many spontaneous "dance parties" that erupt in the middle of the aisles, people are celebrated for acts of kindness. It's no wonder Trader Joe's has an unheard of 4 percent turnover of employees.

Celebrate and reward people for their humanity.

Make-mom-proud companies build their reward systems to celebrate actions of both heart (what we learned at home) and habit (the behavior we are encouraged to continue). Congruence of heart and habit has at its core building an organization that reinforces business behaviors that align with our values.

Employees want to do the right thing; they want to be rewarded for taking the initiative, and acting in a manner that benefits customers. But these actions can become inhibited when motivation doesn't line up. For example, at the investment firm where Joe worked, "customer focus" was a core value of the company. It was stressed in every meeting. A credo to customer service was engraved on the wall. Survey scores were tracked. Yet the metrics discussed and rewarded were sales, average revenue per client, and upsell.

To assist Advisers, they were trained in selling approaches, and given a quota for the number of customers to contact each month, win, and grow. However, Joe wanted to add value and advise his customers, beyond selling. Through spending more time guiding customers, Joe increased his long-term productivity, but he frequently did not meet his monthly customer contact goals. He had to continue to defend his initiative and approach and the growth he'd achieved with his clients each time this occurred.

While each of these meetings ended well for Joe, he was always a little sunk that he wasn't receiving reinforcement for doing the right thing for his clients. Over time, the repeated focus on numbers, without recognition of the quality of his engagements or initiative, led Joe to depart to join another firm.

What Joe craved were reward and recognition for making good independent decisions, and for his skills in innovating and taking the initiative. He's not alone in this desire: Employees asked about contribution and rewards in research conducted by Citigroup and LinkedIn said they would pass up a 20 percent raise in exchange for more control over how they work. Being part of a greater mission and trusted to make decisions and take the initiative was more motivating to them than financial compensation.

When employees are recognized and rewarded for taking the initiative and adding value, they will want to stay. When their behavior and achievements are heralded and celebrated, an elevated company of engaged and energetic employees continue to add value: an elevated company and culture emerges.

So, ask yourself: **Do you celebrate people for their humanity and spirit?**

What follows is a case study about H-E-B, a Texas grocery store chain where trusted store managers grow the business. Beloved by its customers and its employees, H-E-B has more than ninety thousand partners (employees) at 332 Texas stores and more than ten thousand at 56 stores throughout Mexico. Mentoring and challenging employees and honoring them as assets makes their business thrive.

A Case Study to #MakeMomProud

H-E-B Decided to Honor Its Employees as Assets.

DECISION INTENT: Honor employees as assets. Some retailers might place employees on the spreadsheet as a cost. But at H-E-B, employee "partners" are a valuable asset to be nurtured, developed, rewarded, and recognized for doing the right thing, and taking chances. President and Chief Operating Officer Craig Boyan told the *New York Times*: "So many in retail are competing in the race to the bottom, and people are the largest cost. So it seems logical to cut people, and lots of folks are doing it," he said. "We think that's a trap. We believe the race for the bottom cheapens the American experience. It's bad for the country and bad for companies."

ACTION TO #MAKEMOMPROUD: Investment in partners, and a challenge. In 2016, privately held H-E-B initiated the Partner Stock Plan, a gift from the founding Butt family, who contributed 15 percent of the company to be eventually owned under the plan by H-E-B partners. This is being distributed by stock grants and ongoing contributions based on performance. Firmly rooted in growing by sharing company profits with partners, it is a motivator that elevates the business and the people in it. Because H-E-B partners are passionate about taking care of their families and taking care of their customers, this plan further motivates them to do both.

In addition, as H-E-B makes advances in efficiencies and reducing expenses throughout the business, this plan is seen as an opportunity to redirect those resources to compensation. Boyan challenges partners annually to earn their compensation by challenging the status quo of business practices and being innovative. Partners rise to the occasion, providing H-E-B with ideas to honor the customer, improve the experience, and make the business run more smoothly. Giving true decision making to the stores and partners in each, they feel ownership and pride in customizing each of their community experiences. Finally, to ensure true collaboration, H-E-B invests in team and store success rewards and incentives. Individual incentives were abandoned because they led to individual competition rather than the H-E-B core values of collaboration and partnership.

H-E-B honors employees as assets of the business. #MakeMomProud.

IMPACT: H-E-B has held a long-term position on *Forbes*'s 100 Best Places to Work list—one of the perennial honorees on that list. As Texas's largest privately held employer, they grow by honoring more than a hundred thousand partners. One partner, Leslie Sweet, H-E-B director of public affairs in Central Texas, summed this up: "I learn life lessons of how to be a better person from the leadership of H-E-B almost every day. And here comes another big learning—give people your trust, responsibility, and generosity and expect good results to come."

THE MOM LENS

Rewards That Are in Sync with Company Values #MakeMomProud.

H-E-B grocery stores is an irreplaceable fixture in the lives of the customers because it recognizes and rewards honorable, gutsy, and noble people who do the right thing.

> ## Do You Reward Acts and Behavior That Would Make Mom Proud?
>
> *Are Congruence of Heart and Habit Celebrated?*

Nurture Memory Creators.

Give employees the emotional high of being a memory maker.

"THIS IS MY FAVORITE DAY OF THE YEAR."

First they saw one red boot. Was it Spider-Man? Then they got a peek of the tail end of a cape. Superman?! Then there they both were. Superman and Spider-Man were both rappelling down the windows in front of them, washing their hospital room windows.

Every year, sick kids in hospitals around the world rush from their hospital beds and exam rooms to "high five" the superhero window washers making their way down the building in front of their very eyes. Then these superhero men and women meet with the kids and give them a memory they soon won't forget. These "everyday" people become heroes to the kids.

Each of those window-washer superheroes get an emotional "return on investment" in delivering memories to sick kids. They say: "It's one thing I look forward to doing all year." "It kind of takes their [the kids'] minds off what they're really [there] for." "They come running up to the glass. They're just excited to see you." "All the guys had tears of joy in their eyes behind the costumes—it was very touching and overwhelming how excited the children were." In giving of themselves, they receive.

This is the same emotional high that employees in organizations get when they are enabled and encouraged to do the same: become memory creators for customers. The emotional high of delivering a positive memory for a customer becomes their reward for giving someone joy, relief, or care. And it is addictive.

Are you nurturing a company of memory makers?

When we are encouraged to think of someone else's emotions and take action to turn a situation around for them, it lifts us up. And the result is that the memory maker's reward is great, if not greater, than the receiver's.

Enabling 'memory makers' is a deliberate choice for the make-mom-proud companies. It can't be achieved through a memo with the words "BE A MEMORY MAKER." Honoring people to put a little bit of themselves into each interaction and deliver a memory is a company-wide commitment to resources and people. The Ritz-Carlton, for example, considers all of its forty thousand employees to be "memory makers."

Professor and Nobel Prize winner Daniel Kahneman is considered the "memory guru" by many. His writing and research have clarified the importance of memory and why it elevates companies and their people when they embrace memory creation as pivotal. People don't "choose between experiences," he simplified for all of us, "we choose between memories of experiences."

Make-mom-proud companies stand out because they think about the experiences they want their customers to remember—and come back for. They go out of their way to understand where their customers are emotionally. And they give employees the education, opportunity, and ability to act on those emotions.

For example, consider the emotionally charged memory that an insurance company customer has when he's told that, unfortunately, his claim has been denied. There are two memories that the customer can walk away from in this situation. Memory one: "That was painful, they denied my claim, they don't care about me." Memory two: "That was disappointing, but they took the time to let me know why. I'm not glad about the outcome, but I feel taken care of and honored as a customer."

Memory two took someone deliberately starting with the customer and his emotions and how he would feel in being turned down. While the claim outcome for the customer is the same in both situations, memory two leaves the customer with a positive memory about the company and its people. **Do you deliver memories you'd want your mom to have?**

Creating a company of memory makers is truly a joyful endeavor, as it lets everyone take the initiative and leave their mark with customers and each other. When people are delivering memories beyond businesses processes, their pride is connected with their work. And Mom? Well, of course she's proud.

This next story I thought important to share because of the emerging trend in some places to lean extensively on technology alone to drive customer contact and, therefore, also memory creation. Danny Meyer, CEO of the Union Square Hospitality Group (USHG), believes that technology is an enabler for humans delivering memories but that it should never take its place. Technology enhances human contact in his establishments, but it will never replace it.

Enjoy his take on enabling people to be memory makers. And ask yourself, "How deliberate are we in becoming a memory-creation company?"

A Case Study to #MakeMomProud

Restaurateur Danny Meyer Decided That People, Not Technology, Deliver Memories.

DECISION INTENT: People first. Technology second. To have an impact that people remember, Union Square first calls upon a platform Meyer developed called the *Hospitality Quotient*, to place people who are kind and optimistic, intellectually curious, have an amazing work ethic, a high degree of empathy, and are self-aware. It is only after these requirements are met, in Meyer's opinion, that technology can and should have an impact. This formula puts people in the position to use technology to its greatest advantage, in Meyer's opinion: to enable an even greater degree of high touch. Meyer puts technology in the shoes of enabling "human beings who actually have a beating heart and who are caring people to achieve a *greater* degree of hospitality."

ACTION TO #MAKEMOMPROUD: The right people with the right technology = memories.

Putting people first and technology second drives the entire operation within the Union Square Hospitality Group. And that blend puts people in a position to deliver memories. Here's a great example that illustrates how an early Union Square Hospitality restaurant, Shake Shack, and technology deliver the magic:

Many foodies build vacations around going on what has been coined a "Danny dine-around." Entire vacations are planned around hitting all of Meyer's restaurants in New York. One couple who had meticulously planned their dine-around trip were, unfortunately, sadly disappointed when their final visit—to the Shake Shack at JFK airport (right?!)—was not in the terminal they were departing from. Crestfallen, they tweeted their dismay . . . and that's when the memory makers kicked into gear. Shake Shack employees scanning tweets immediately picked it up, made the couple meals, and rushed them to their gate. The astounded couple could smell the burgers before they saw the guys running toward them. Helpful, hopeful, and happy plus technology = memories.

Union Square Hospitality Hires and Nurtures Memory Makers. #MakeMomProud.

IMPACT: Union Square Hospitality Group restaurants consistently defy the odds of the restaurant business: a shocking 60 percent don't survive the first year, and 80 percent fail within five years. Danny Meyer says that what makes diners return—or not—is how they were made to *feel*, which makes finding those memory makers a top priority. USHG's turnover rate for full-time employees is about 19 percent annually, compared with an industry average of 27 percent. It has grown to be one of the five largest restaurant companies based in New York City, according to Technomic Inc., which estimates the privately held group's annual revenue at between $250 million and $500 million.

THE MOM LENS

Nurturing and Enabling "Memory Makers" #MakesMomProud.

Union Square Hospitality hires people for their humanity, guiding them to focus on how customers feel when seated at their tables, and delivering memories that stay long after the meal is over.

Do You Nurture Memory Makers?

Can They Deliver Memories You'd Want Your Mom to Have?

Summarizing
"Be the Person I Raised You to Be."

Make-mom-proud companies seek people whose values align with what they want their companies to stand for. And then they enable them to bring that version of themselves to work. Selecting who will, and will not, become members of these companies is job one. But after that, the focus is to help them to prosper. As a result, people are content. They feel that their work is valued. They have a purpose that transcends individual action items: improving customers' lives. These companies take deliberate actions in order to:

* Honor the dignity of customers' lives.

* Nurture, develop, and trust employees.

* Enable employees to extend grace, joy, and memories.

* Reward and develop congruence of heart and habit.

In this chapter, we thought of Mom as she interacted with the human beings of your company. Did she feel cared for? Were her needs understood? Was she honored as a valued customer? Was she helped without judgment or bias? Did her emotional needs get met? Were the people who served her content in their work? Beyond Mom, how would all of your customers answer these questions? Is a culture of caring consistent across your organization?

TAKE ACTION!

*Would you earn kudos from Mom in how you
honor, value, and enable employees?*

Chapter 6, "Stop the Shenanigans!," will help you evaluate where you are today. It will serve as a mirror test for you to work through with your company and teams. There you will find each of the opportunities and studies outlined with questions to plot your current state. Your evaluation will help you plan your actions to nudge your company toward where you want it to be.

Please also go to customerbliss.com, where you can find training videos for these stories, the comics, and a leader guide so you can use this material inside your company.

3.

Don't Make Me Feed You Soap!

"My mother had a great deal of trouble with me,
but I think she enjoyed it."

–MARK TWAIN

Raise your hand if you've ever had your mouth washed out with soap, or your mom threatened to do this to you. She used that bar of soap to curb habits that drove her nuts, like when we repeatedly didn't do our homework, clean our rooms, or help around the house. And while this practice (thankfully) is not used much today, we still, unfortunately, do some things in business that make Mom nuts—that, sadly, would warrant her bar of soap in our mouths.

This chapter is dedicated to getting rid of those bubbles.

We've got to get rid of the "wobbly" things done to customers, often unintentionally, that nonetheless creep into customer experiences. These are the moments that make it harder for customers to get things done. They lead to a "dukes up" approach as customers fend for themselves. And they make it hard for employees to deliver value.

This is our opportunity to (finally) remove what makes it hard to be a customer: waiting, complexity, uncertainty, and sometimes fear. To show up more humanly in moments when customers might feel like they have to navigate our organization chart to get the help and service they crave. We need to eliminate the challenges to how we provide service, information, and support. Our opportunity is to turn these moments into ones of reliability, respect, and caring.

The Make-mom-proud companies are always on the lookout for "bar of soap" moments they can remove from customers' lives.

For example, Dignity Health, the fifth largest healthcare system in the United States, eliminated a classic "bar of soap" moment in healthcare when they introduced an online ER waiting room for non-life-threatening emergencies. Patients access an app called "Emergency Care Waiting Service," which looks similar to a restaurant-booking app, where they select a convenient location and available time for their emergency-room visit. With this service, they've taken the frustration of waiting out of the waiting-room experience. "No one plans a trip to the emergency department, but it's at those moments patients need kindness the most," the page introducing this service says.

Perhaps such actions are inspired by how CEO Lloyd Dean was raised. "My mother told me three things that have stuck with me and served me well," he said. "One, be willing to stand up for what you believe in. Sometimes that means standing alone, but no matter what, be a person of principles even if it isn't easy. Second, treat others as you want to be treated. And third, be proud of who you are."

Think of your life as a customer. How many "bar of soap" moments do you experience in any given day? How many do your customers experience? Is the story of their lives as your customer seamless, calming, and predictable?

The price of delivering experiences that are *not* seamless, calming, and predictable is expensive. According to Siegel+Gale, brands that don't provide simple experiences are leaving an estimated share of $86 billion on the table. A whopping 64 percent of customers will pay for simpler experiences! This doesn't even factor in the operating cost expended when customers need to contact you for help.

And, of course, all of these painful moments eventually roll onto the feet of your front line. Customers ask: Where is it? How long will it take? Why can't you do that? What does this mean? Why don't you have my records? Why was I charged this fee? Can you waive it? Will you really help me? Can you get me out of this contract? Why have I been on hold for fifteen minutes? Siegel+Gale research also shows that 65 percent of employees at companies who make things simple become champions for that brand—versus 20 percent of employees who work for companies wrought with complexity.

Wringing these "soapy" moments out of your operation won't be easy. But you can start by taking a look at your social media comments, pictures, calls, and chats with your customers. Many of them have bubbles all over them. The fact is that **these experiences are often what we remember** and discuss in social media. They can define our lives as customers.

Here are some of the most common "bar of soap" experiences that define our lives as customers. Along with each are case studies from companies that have flipped these practices on their ears to "Make Mom Proud." A little inspiration right out of the starting gate.

Honor Customers' Time, and Their Clock.

Keep "customer time."

"I'VE HAD BREAKFAST, LUNCH AND A SNACK. I'VE GAINED 15 POUNDS AND THE CABLE GUY IS STILL NOT HERE."

When you honor people's time, when their urgency is your urgency, worry and concern are replaced with peace of mind. The shoulders relax, the dialing and texting and not knowing don't begin. For example, this doozy of an experience below is one that has affected all of our lives as customers. Raise your hand if it hasn't. I want to know you—you've lived your life well.

Would you give your mom a four-hour window in which you *might* show up for a visit? Of course you wouldn't. But this has happened to all of us when receiving services. Building in a four-hour window makes it easier on the company to schedule, but says to the customer: our time and priorities matter more than yours. According to a survey conducted by CNN Money, 58 percent of all Americans said they have waited for in-home appointments, for the cable guy and other in-home service workers, an average of four and a half hours.

That's what happened to Mary, a healthcare worker at a Minneapolis hospital. When her refrigerator went on the fritz, she was given a four-hour window in which the repairman would show up. "Okay, he'll show up within the first hour, with any luck," she thought. No dice and no luck. Needing to know when she could get back to work, she called the 800 number, waited on hold for fifteen minutes, and then was told a representative would send a note to her repairman and he'd text her back. Hope!

Her hope was dashed when no text came, and the waiting began again. Her repairman finally showed up in the final twenty minutes of the four-hour window. And when Mary said, "You were supposed to be here and done within the four-hour window," he replied, "No, that's the time when it was promised I'd show up!"

Keep "customer time."
Make their clock, your clock.

For all of us, actions, not promises, equal the measure of integrity and respect. Honoring customers' time will earn their rave. Customers will remember you for the service delivered, and not the energy expended to receive it.

The impact of making people wait, especially for in-home services, has consequences that go beyond an unfortunate memory that sticks and is shared on social media. CNNMoney research referenced earlier also revealed that many of the people who waited for in-home appointments lost wages waiting. Half of respondents had to use a sick day or a vacation day to wait for service providers. This waiting game continues beyond the cable guy to customers in nearly every industry.

In fact, in Israel, in an effort to require repair technicians to show respect for customers waiting for them, the Knesset, Israel's unicameral parliament, is endeavoring to pass the "technician's law." If passed, it will impose fees on companies who show up for a repair an hour late or more than promised. Customers all around the world are waiting to be served.

The make-mom-proud companies wrap their operations around respecting customers' time. They don't ever want customers' lives to revolve around *their* schedule. For example, Amazon Prime leader Stephenie Landry says that they focus their entire customer experience around answering two questions: "Do you have what I want, and can you get it to me when I need it?" Many cable companies have recently started to follow suit, honoring customers' time with short appointment windows and reliable communication. Bravo!

This is our opportunity to become reliable for customers by honoring their time and telling them (preferably before they ask), the answer to these questions: "Where is it, when will it get here, and how long do I have to wait?" Do YOU honor customers' time and their clock?

This next case study focuses on another kind of waiting: waiting in line for services. This story highlights the ingenuity of Sweetgreen Restaurants, which wants you to get your salad fast, but with a healthy dose of humanity. Sweetgreen tackled the standing-in-line experience with aplomb, personality, and grace. And like other make-mom-proud companies, they wire in technology to enhance, not replace, the connections between their business, their people, and their customers.

A Case Study to #MakeMomProud

Sweetgreen Decided You Need Your Salad in Less Than Ten Minutes.

DECISION INTENT: Don't make people choose between healthy and fast. Sweetgreen is a fast-casual restaurant company on a mission to serve food that is delicious, healthy, affordable, and *fast*. Their goal was to *"bridge the gap between health and convenience"* because *"we all have better things to do than stand in line."* Sweetgreen partners with local farms so that every ingredient offered in its salads and wraps *are constantly changing with the seasons.* They're the answer for people who don't want to trade healthy eating for a fast meal. Sweetgreen's operation honors their customers' time without compromising the quality of their products or service.

ACTION TO #MAKEMOMPROUD: Intimacy at Scale—speedy service and a human connection. Sweetgreen didn't want to show up as the typical fast-food impersonal assembly line. So your salad isn't handed off to an assembly line, and neither are you. Customers and employees forge a personal, human connection as they build each customer's meal. Investments in employee training, equipment, and process ensures each customer experience is personalized experience, and fast. Initially moving a customer from line to eating their meal in ten minutes, eight minutes is now the goal.

To achieve this, they now offer a mobile app so customers can order ahead remotely. This lets customers skip the line altogether, but not the personality of the Sweetgreen experience. Sweetgreen's app is as human and intuitive as possible. Working to mimic the personal and caring guidance customers receive in line in the store, it lets you build the salad of your dreams, guiding you with nutritional nudges. You can save your favorites and order them again within five taps. Cashless ordering speeds things along even more. And they are working on what they've coined ASAP ordering—giving customers real-time tracking and an animated image of your salad bowl going from empty to filled with your meal—giving you a time when it's ready for you to grab it. Any way you order from Sweetgreen, they work to ensure it is always served with a healthy dose of humanity.

Sweetgreen Delivers Humanity and Salads. #MakeMomProud.

IMPACT: Started in 2007, Sweetgreen has grown swiftly to seventy-two restaurants and 1,700 employees. Still in its start-up phase, Sweetgreen has raised nearly $100 million primarily from venture capitalists. Keeping focused on employees to deliver that human experience, Sweetgreen's employee benefits include paid parental leave for mothers and fathers, and Sweetgreen Impact Hours, which is up to five paid hours of leave to "volunteer, participate in community events, or work at a farm."

THE MOM LENS

Honoring Customers' Time and Their Schedule #MakesMomProud.

Sweetgreen is on a mission to deliver healthy food fast, but with a dose of humanity. Their zest for speed is grounded in respect for customers' time, and their commitment that "fast" food doesn't mean missing out on a healthy meal, served by people who care.

Do You Honor Customers' Time, and Their Clock?

Is Your Business Run on "Customer Time"?

Take the Monkey Off the Customer's Back.

End service exhaustion.

"KEEP CALLING US TO CHECK ON YOUR LOST LUGGAGE. IN THE MEANTIME, ENJOY THAT STIPEND TO RE-BUY ALL YOUR VACATION CLOTHES."

In our lives as customers, when things go south and we need help, sometimes our own fortitude in fending for ourselves determines the outcome. The "extra-mile customer" who has the gusto to call and call, and search, and act as a private eye, and put the pieces together, and make copies, and send files, and return receipts gets the worm. The monkey is put on the customers' back, and *service exhaustion* is the result. We're glad for the outcome we achieved, but don't know if we have it in us to do it again.

This occurs as customer requests for support or information or assistance are met with a set of actions (monkeys) that the customer must take or wait for or persist in checking up on. And the customer who can't keep calling back or searching for answers is just as worn out as the "extra mile customer." Globally, 56 percent of respondents in Microsoft's 2017 State of Global Customer Service Report have ceased doing business with a brand because of poor service experiences. **Would you make your mom do work to get good service,** which you could have easily done for her?

End Service Exhaustion!

Make-mom-proud companies think about all of the steps and the people and the processes that it takes for customers to interact with them. And they resist layering work on customers. **They work to remove the monkeys from customers' backs.**

Healthcare is one industry that delivers a lot of those monkeys. We are often left to our own devices to ensure that our health records travel with us as we move to different health-care providers. The Mayo Clinic calls this "the burden of treatment." And because many record-keeping systems are not yet connected, we are still hand carrying X-rays and test results and filling out numerous forms ourselves to get them transferred from one physician's office to the next.

For those who have numerous medications to manage, the maze is even more complex. Patients have to connect the dots to ensure that medications prescribed by different physicians don't cause adverse reactions.

The Pharmacy Home Project is a make-mom-proud action that supports the elderly especially prone to medication complexity. The service in North Carolina run by the Community Care of North Carolina guides these patients to help them manage their medications. They travel home with these folks, examine what's in their medicine cabinets, and help them navigate the complicated maze of various medications prescribed by separate physicians, preventing potentially adverse reactions or overmedication.

While we might *expect* "monkeys" in complex industries such as healthcare, it's always a bit startling when they are layered on us where we least expect them; when the solution, we thought, should have been so simple. Monkeys pop up in every industry.

After two weeks of wearing his new watch, Steven's watch strap broke. He called the store he'd bought it from to find out how to get it repaired. They told him they didn't know for sure but suggested that he go to their corporate site and fill out a claim form, then copy it, scan it, and send it to them. He took these actions, but why did these actions fall to Steven? Why didn't the store advocate on his behalf? After a week and no word from the store, he called to check on the status of his claim. They couldn't find his form, and asked him to send it again. They would get back to him in a week. They made him do the work again. A week later after not hearing from the store, Steven called once again to speak to a store manager, who said he would look into it. He never heard back from this manager. It was up to Steven to reach out to them—more monkeys.

Finally, three weeks later, Steven heard from a store representative who gave him the name of a local shop where he could take the watch to be repaired. But the store would not pay for the $100 repair. Steven, at this point, said he'd just rather return the watch. The store could not complete his return, he was told. Instead, he was directed to the customer care number to process his return. Instead of advocating for Steven, the company made him fend for himself, all the way through returning the faulty watch that he had purchased from them.

This cycle that Steven experienced, where every customer need or request was met with a new set of actions he had to take to advocate for himself, is at the root of service exhaustion. Every question Steven asked resulted in an action he had to take. Then each of his actions required a follow-up to determine whether any action had been taken on his behalf. Even the final outcome demanded an action Steven had to take. Did you count the number of monkeys there?

The make-mom-proud companies rethink how they do business with customers to get rid of the extra work they push to them. They know that the more monkeys they put on customers' backs, the more customers will talk about the experience. Not because of the joy, but because of the work required to advocate on their own behalf.

As you think of Steven's story, think about customer experiences with your company. What monkeys have you taken off your customers' backs? Are there any monkeys that remain?

Below is a story about Virginia Mason Medical Center in Seattle, which has removed the "burden of treatment" from its patients with back pain. Previously patients had the burden of scheduling all of their separate appointments, tests, and caregivers; the redesigned experience unites caregivers, tests, diagnostics, and therapy to make it seamless and coordinated. The goal in redesigning this service was not only to fix backs, but also to take monkeys off them (sorry, couldn't resist).

A Case Study to #MakeMomProud

Virginia Mason Decided to Take the Healthcare Monkey Off Your Back.

DECISION INTENT: Ease the burden of care for our patients. Healthcare piles a lot of monkeys onto our backs. As health-care consumers we are asked to gather for our primary physician or the specialty doc or the insurance agency all of the pieces each one needs. This form, that form. This approval, then that approval. See Doctor A before you see Doctor C, no Doctor D. We must somehow figure out how to piece it all together, see the right doctor(s) and, hopefully, get insurance coverage. That's because often healthcare is organized by its own set of silos by physician specialty or hospital or system, many of which don't integrate. The burden of care is ours. To really serve our needs as patients, health-care providers need to unite to help us solve our ailment—versus making us unite them all ourselves.

ACTION TO #MAKEMOMPROUD: 206-41-SPINE. This is the phone number to call at Virginia Mason Medical Center in Seattle if you have lower back pain. Starting with the ailment rather than their organization chart, this health-care group unites a team of experts to provide their patient "customers" a one-stop shop to help them heal. And those patients immediately experience a totally different approach, one that is centered on *them*. That's because Virginia Mason's practice leaders took the time to understand all of the rigmarole that someone with back pain usually has to go through. And then they got rid of it.

The Seattle Virginia Mason integrated practice unit is organized around you and your back. On your first visit, made the day you call, you see what they call a spine team. This is a physical therapist/physician team that collaborates on your condition immediately to set you on a course of treatment, often beginning with therapy that day. No bouncing, no new appointments. No monkey. For people with more extreme back pain issues, they are connected with partners who then take the patients to an advanced level of care. These customers are not handed off to fend for themselves.

Virginia Mason's Spine Clinic Provides Complete Care. #MakeMomProud.

IMPACT: As a result of redesigning the processes of care, Virginia Mason eliminated MRIs that were prescribed unnecessarily. They now quickly identify patients who require an MRI, and get the majority who do not have rapid access to physical therapy and return to work. In the last published data, compared with regional averages, patients at Virginia Mason's Spine Clinic miss fewer days of work (4.3 versus 9 per episode) and need fewer physical therapy visits (4.4 versus 8.8). MRI scans to evaluate low back pain has decreased by 23 percent since the clinic's launch, in 2005. This more efficient model of care increases revenue through increased productivity and reduction of unnecessary expenses, fees, and processing. Hospitals across the United States are emulating Virginia Mason's system.

THE MOM LENS

Removing the Burden
of Doing Business
#MakesMomProud.

Virginia Mason's Spine Clinic puts all the pieces together for its customers so they don't have to. Instead, it shoulders the work of uniting caregivers, actions, and records.

Do You Take the Monkeys Off Your Customers' Back?

Can You Reduce Service Exhaustion?

Don't Leave Customers in the Dark.

Communicate for peace of mind.

"WOW, NO COMPUTER VIRUSES, NO POP-UP ADS, NO SPAM.
...BECAUSE THERE IS NO ELECTRICITY."

When customers need you, are you there? Are you actively communicating when the unexpected happens and the power goes out, flights are canceled, appointments must be rescheduled, or shipments are late? Do you proactively reach out when service is disrupted? Do you get to customers before the tweets and the calls for help begin?

We are human, and in our companies disruptions will occur. Customers get that. What they need is the confidence that you remember they're out there. The make-mom-proud companies let customers know that they are watching out for them at these moments. They are walking in their shoes, and taking what's happening to them personally.

Karen and her family felt pretty forgotten when they lost power during the final snowstorm of the year in Ohio last March (always in March!). They received no communication after Karen registered a notice of their outage on the power company website and left a message on the company's computer-generated voice mail system. Two days later, there was still no power, and no word on what was happening. The next afternoon, without any notice or communication, the power went back on. Karen's family had spent three cold, uninformed evenings in the dark, and lost the contents of their refrigerator and freezer.

Would you leave your mom in the dark, without any information, when her power was out? Of course you wouldn't. So, why does this sometimes happen to customers?

When things don't go as planned, customers want to know that you are thinking of them. There is nothing worse than being in the dark with no updates and no information and a feeling that you are alone. They don't want to be forgotten. Of course, companies don't set out to create these disruptions. But planning and executing smooth customer recovery experiences is not always part of every business operation.

Deliver Peace of Mind.

Make-mom-proud companies huddle hourly, daily, and nightly to know, before customers tell them, what is happening in their lives. They call, they post, they chat, and they tweet with the updates and information. They stay in touch and keep customers out of the dark. They give them peace of mind that they are working on their behalf.

Delivering that peace of mind benefits both customers and the companies who work to provide it. Seventy-seven percent of global consumers think more favorably of a company when they receive proactive alerts and notifications from it.

In situations when websites crash, packages aren't delivered, deadlines are missed, or service suddenly stops, the make-mom-proud companies stand out because they've built a "customer recovery" system to anticipate these occurrences; they recognize them when they are happening, and they jump into action and start communicating with customers. *This* is what creates raving fans in those moments when customers are stressed, worried, and afraid. They earn the right to their customers' stories and to their rave in the marketplace.

Do you take disruptions in customers' lives personally? Is your company poised to unite, huddle, communicate, and act? Do you make sure customers know that you know they require your help—and that you're on it? In fact, research reveals that if you put customers in a hole and then dig them out, you may have an even more devoted customer if you do it well. (Not a test worth conducting.)

In this next story, you'll learn how CenterPoint Energy in Houston delivers proactive communication that customers thank them for and rave about. Their proactive approach and ingenuity give great examples of experience redesign blending with technology and communication. As a result, they have elevated communication as a *product* that they want customers to count on.

A Case Study to #MakeMomProud

CenterPoint Energy Decided to Communicate, Communicate, Communicate.

DECISION INTENT: Deliver peace of mind to customers while restoring normalcy to their lives. "Who would have thought that communicating to a customer that their power is out, and why, would be our highest rated 'product' in our utility?" Gregory Knight, chief customer officer at CenterPoint Energy in Houston, says their dedication to these actions are setting them apart and bonding them with customers.

ACTION TO #MAKEMOMPROUD: Make proactive communication and knowledge a "product." Recognizing that this is an industry that gives customers emotional angst from not knowing why the power went out or when it will be back on, Center-Point Energy started with customers' lives and their emotions. They created an empathy map to understand the feelings and needs of both customers and the front line that serves them. Through this map and many conversations, they gained clarity on this simple fact: *Not* knowing what's happening makes people nuts! Lack of communication is the root of customer unrest, worry, and fear.

In the end, customers want to know "when did my power get interrupted, why did this happen, and when will my life get back to normal?" That is why CenterPoint Energy got C-suite funding to make communication a "product" to help customers know they are thinking of them. It is as important as any other service they invest in.

For years, CenterPoint offered outage information on an online map. But now, the company is proactively reaching out. When-

ever possible, customers are now automatically enrolled in a proactive communication experience that is yielding increased trust—especially when the bad stuff happens. For example, when the power goes out, they receive by phone, text, or email:

- A message verifying power outage, the expected outage time line, and actions to stay safe.
- Follow-up communications updated with the estimated time to restore.
- When the power is back on, customers receive a message confirming the restoration.
- "Hot spot" customers hit with multiple outages receive additional messaging indicating that the company knows what they are going through. They are provided a contact for assistance, and communicated with when the issue or issues have been resolved.

CenterPoint Energy Knows You Need to Know. #MakeMomProud.

IMPACT: Gregg Knight told me, "We need to show up as caring, responsive and as a good solution if we want to move from a company that simply satisfies customers to one that inspires loyalty, advocacy, and trust." It appears that their efforts are getting them there. Customers who enrolled in the Power Alert Service give it a 91 percent satisfaction rating. And Cogent Reports, which conducted the largest benchmarking study on utilities, names them consistently as a national leader in brand trust and community engagement.

THE MOM LENS

Keeping Customers Informed and Out of the Dark #MakesMomProud.

CenterPoint Energy delivers proactive communication when the power goes out. They remove the emotional angst of not knowing, and instead inform, communicate, and support.

Do You Take Disruptions in Customers' Lives Personally?

How Do You Keep Them Apprised, and Give Them Peace of Mind?

Enable Graceful Departures.

A graceful departure may lead to an eventual return.

"NO, HE'S NOT BREAKING UP WITH A CLINGY GIRLFRIEND,
HE'S TRYING TO CANCEL HIS PHONE PLAN."

"Ride our bike for 50 days; if you don't like it, return it, no questions asked." "Cancel your subscription for those razor blades—it's OK, we understand." "Try our bank for a little while, and if you don't like how we help, we will send you off with £100; thank you, please come back when we can serve you again."

These three honest, simple, and easy terms of engagement are brought to you by three customer-driven companies: First, Roll bicycles decided that road time and assistance in helping you receive, build, and take care of that bike is why they want you to stay. No contract can convince you of that. Roll bicycle customers get fifty days to ride and decide, then return. Next, Dollar Shave Club decided that great value blades, whimsy, and service are their glue. They won't keep you captive with a contract. And finally, UK-based First Direct Bank, which makes it easy to switch to them, gives you £100 as a farewell gift if they're not your cup of tea. These companies won't pen you in. Delivering value to you is what motivates them.

Make-mom-proud companies would rather keep your business with service and value, not contract terms. On the other hand, some companies just don't want to let you go.

Kevin purchased a one-year software package of services, expecting from the description of the service offering that he could end the subscription after that year if he needed to. What he didn't know was that he had signed up for an automatic-renew cycle, and billing automatically began after his first year ran out. The fine print said that he could only cancel within month eleven of the twelve-month subscription.

When he figured this out, Kevin called customer service to cancel, but was informed that the automatic renewal was irreversible. The company offered him a solution: he could pay a cancellation fee equal to 50 percent of the new contract he had unwittingly just signed up for. He ended his twenty-year relationship with the company.

Would you charge your mom a penalty for canceling her subscription with you? Or would you take the opportunity to learn why she's leaving, and thank her for her business?

A graceful departure may lead to an eventual return.

As customers, our lives and needs change, and sometimes we just don't need something anymore. Maybe it's a monthly subscription we signed up for and forgot, and now we have a lifetime supply of vitamins. (True story.) Or we need to switch cable providers or our phone plan. Or opt out of a subscription. At these times, enabling a graceful departure, unintuitive as it may sound, can lead to an eventual return.

When you assist customers and provide them with all of the ins and outs of canceling, the fine print involved, the possible "Gotcha!" moments lurking, and the billing implications, you get a customer grateful for how you conducted yourself.

Pronet, a company that offers residential and commercial security solutions in Turkey, for example, recently reimagined their customer departure experience. They simplified the experience from having to speak to four different teams, to honoring the departing customer with one single point of contact, creating a "super-agent role" emboldened to "do the right thing" for customers as they departed. Rather than never wanting to talk to Pronet again, the previous sentiment of departing customers, this new experience opens the door for customers to return.

Think of the last personal breakup you might have had. If it went well, there was an opportunity to remain friends. If not, the breakup experience validated the reasons for letting go—and your feet couldn't take you away from the situation fast enough. In many ways, leaving a company has the same emotional impact.

And bad breakups also tend to live long lives on social media. When customers have to jump through hoops to leave you, they will tell everyone they know. And the harder the departure, just like that breakup, the more people the customer will tell about it. The cost to the company multiplies. A well-handled departure can earn a future return. But a challenging departure closes that door.

Casper, a company that sells mattresses, makes graceful departures their mission. Casper wants to become the "Nike of sleep" by creating a new experience for resting easy in your life. They are driven more by delivering value than by enforcing rules that pen customers in and hold them captive. As a result, Casper wants you to take their bed for a long test-drive—so you can really get to know them. They want you to stay only if you sleep easier because of them. And if not, well, read on.

A Case Study to #MakeMomProud

Casper Decided to Let You "Sleep on It" for One Hundred Days.

DECISION INTENT: Take the rigmarole out of buying a bed. Casper launched in April 2014 with a single product: one bed. Its five founders had all gone through the rigmarole of buying beds, as we all have, trying to navigate the showroom, the many options, and the pitches and pressure to close the sale. Cofounder Neil Parikh said in an early interview with *Inc.* magazine, "The salesmen talk fast; the choices are overwhelming and the prices are hefty. Yet everyone needs a mattress. . . . It's worse than buying a used car." The result? These five guys, Philip Krim, Jeff Chapin, Neil Parikh, Luke Sherwin, and Gabriel Flateman, banded together to "disrupt the sleep industry." Then they wanted to go further, to create a whole industry around sleep. Their goal: become the "Nike of sleep." They knew that to eventually achieve this goal, they had to break and rebuild the entire experience of trying, buying, and even returning a bed.

ACTION TO #MAKEMOMPROUD: One hundred days to return their mattress. Casper's one hundred days return service came out of this fact: it is nutty that people make a decision they live with for years, by lying on a mattress in a store for two to three minutes. And who is comfortable lying on a bed with your shoes on while the salesman keeps asking you what you think? As part of their crusade to make buying a bed more humane, Casper gives customers one hundred days to sleep on their bed *at home*. Then if it's not right for them, Casper will pick it up for free. No restocking fee, and no guilt. Why would Casper do this? They don't consider a bed a one-time transaction. They are in it for the relationship. They urge customers to call and chat, and more than half of them do that before buying a bed. They keep track of customer data and stay in touch—because they aren't selling beds; they're helping you get a better night's sleep.

Casper Let's You Sleep Easy. #MakeMomProud.

IMPACT: Casper has grown from $0 sales in 2013 to more than $500 million in four years. As of this writing, Target stores had bid a cool $1 billion to buy the company, but instead became a partner, investing $75 million in the company. Casper was the second-place contender for *Inc.* magazine's Company of the Year in 2016. They are now in both West Elm and Target stores, where customers can touch and feel and, yes, lie on that bed a bit before they buy. The hundred-day return still applies. Casper has become the largest online brand selling beds in the world. Finally, with their "no strings attached" approach, customer returns remain exceedingly low—7 percent or less.

THE MOM LENS

Letting Customers Depart Gracefully #MakesMomProud.

Casper mattresses generously gives customers one hundred days to try their beds, and a painless and dignified departure experience if theirs is just not the bed for them.

Do You Let Customers Depart Gracefully, with Dignity Intact?

Would Your Departure Experience Earn an Eventual Return?

Make It Easy to Get Help.

Be available to support customers' lives.

"YOUR CALL IS VERY IMPORTANT TO US.
PEASE CONTINUE TO HOLD."

When we need help, time is compressed. We need help *n-o-w*! When that help comes swiftly, wrapped in a caring "voice" (by phone, internet chat, face-to-face, or social service), we feel a little saved. We can get back to what we were supposed to be doing before our lives were interrupted. This is our opportunity: to make it EASY for customers to get our attention and assistance.

Oh, but the tussle we go through at times.

Susan was directed to an 800 number to get an authorization for a prescription for her son. She had fifteen minutes between meetings, so she thought she'd make the call. When the phone rang immediately, she was relieved. Susan was then greeted with an automated phone tree asking her to input her insurance information and name and choose from a tree of seven options, and the reason she was calling. Susan was then passed on to another operator who asked her to repeat the same information that she had just punched in, verified her information, and then placed her on hold for six minutes to review her account. **Would you put your mom through your phone tree,** before solving her problem?

When the operator returned back to the line, Susan was asked four more pieces of information and then put on hold for four more minutes. Each time on hold, Susan heard ads for the company's products and services. Next time the operator returned, she said that she needed to hand Susan's case over to a specialist. After six minutes on hold, Susan was put into an automated phone tree asking her to input all of the information that she had originally entered. Susan now knew she'd miss her next meeting, but didn't want to begin again. When the specialist answered four minutes later, she asked Susan to repeat the same information, then placed her on hold for seven minutes, and finally returned with an approval.

According to the Dialog Direct Customer Rage Study, the number one phrase that makes everyone crazy is this doozy: "Your call is very important to us. Please continue to hold." Ahem, if it is, then why am I on hold? Isn't that what we always ask ourselves? "I'm getting old while I'm waiting on hold" feels oh so true. But this is not just about being on hold. It's about availability, flexibility in how companies can be reached, and swiftness of care. With the increasing number of customers opting for self-service, **it's never been more important to be available,** and solve customers' problems when they reach out to you.

Let your availability reflect how much you care.

Make-mom-proud companies adapt their availability to fit customers' needs. They are flexible, available, offer swift human care when desired, and provide the right resources for customers in need.

In every type of business vertical, they let customers know "We are here for you." Discover Card recently enabled customers to reach service agents via real-time texting, eliminating the need to stay logged onto the Discover app to receive assistance. Agents also have access to customers' full messaging history. Ochsner Medical Center in New Orleans has built an electronic medical record system and corresponding apps that record patient behaviors, such as their steps and sleep, and their test results right into their medical records. These then transmit immediately to doctors via Apple Watches to swiftly respond to patients in need of care. Seattle Children's Hospital now makes "house calls" via video call for kids too sick to leave home.

At clothing retailer Bonobos, when call volume spikes, people all around the company trained as "white belt ninjas" (junior to their regular full-time customer ninjas who handle calls) engage with customers swiftly. Hyatt Hotels invested two years to reduce the number of keystrokes required of your hotel clerk from 143 to 3 on a tablet, so he or she could spend more time taking care of you and your needs.

Are you ready to make being *available* synonymous with how much you *care* for customers? Think of customers working that phone tree, on hold listening to music, waiting for chat to start, or watching their phone for your Twitter response. Build your version of availability and care, fueled by "Customer Rescue Artists" who will help you earn the right to business growth.

Up next is a company beloved by "pet parents." Its reliable service and its reliable availability have engendered trust in its customers. Chewy.com knows the moments for peace of mind, and it has wrapped its experience around delivering it. **It makes "available" synonymous with "care."**

A Case Study to #MakeMomProud

Chewy.com Decided to Deliver Reliable Care for "Pet Parents."

DECISION INTENT: Be there whenever pet parents need us. If you have a pet, it's likely that you have become a pet parent. Your pet is a member of your family, and you seek out the best of everything for it. Most important, you want smart, knowledgeable people guiding you to the right food, equipment, and care. And when your pet is not himself, a swift response and personalized assistance by someone who's knowledgeable, and who cares.

ACTION TO #MAKEMOMPROUD: Always available, always informed service. At Chewy.com service starts with your life as a pet parent. "Chewtopians" answer your call twenty-four hours a day, 7 days a week, 365 days of the year. When you call Chewy, it's answered within five seconds. And a live and trained person answers the phone, ready to banter, talk about your pet, or answer a complex question about pet food or pet care. These are pet lovers and owners, trained in all of the products. And they share the bond you have with your pet. There are no call length limits, and you will *never* be handed off to someone else. Reps are trained to help you from start to finish—with you and your pet as their only priority. These folks take an average of seven thousand unique calls a day, during which your pet's name, profile, and needs are recorded in a companywide database, so there is a "memory" of both of you.

Prefer live chat? Live chat calls are answered within six seconds by a human. Emails are answered within twenty minutes with a personalized response. Swift social media conversations follow this same pattern. You'll hear back from a "Chewtopian" in less than five minutes when you connect or mention Chewy.com via Instagram, Twitter, Facebook, or YouTube. Swiftness and reliability continue in delivery, with 60 percent of orders delivered overnight.

Chewy's intent is to nurture a relationship based on trust, personal care, and truly knowing you and your pet. Customers receive handwritten holiday cards. A beloved pet's passing is often met with a bouquet sent to the grieving pet parent.

Chewy.com Is Always There for Pet Parents. #MakeMomProud.

IMPACT: At this writing, 2017 sales were estimated at $2 billion, from $26 million in 2012, Chewy.com's first full year of business. Chewy.com fulfills 51 percent of online pet food sales, per 1010data. To give you perspective, Amazon.com fulfills 35 percent. In 2017, they received the Stevie Award for Customer Service Department of the Year. Also in 2017, PetSmart acquired them for roughly $3.5 billion for their ability to nurture and grow zealot online customers. "Paws crossed" that Chewy.com will continue its unique way of doing business and continue to thrive.

THE MOM LENS

Making It Easy for Customers to Get Help #MakesMomProud.

Chewy gives pet parents always available, always informed service. From people who care—and who know the answers! They take the time to invest in people who know, and in knowing you and your pet.

Do You Make It Easy to Get Help?

Is Your Availability a Reflection of How Much You Care?

Stop the Customer Hot Potato.

Show up as a team to your customer.

THE MORTGAGE BERMUDA TRIANGLE

hot po·ta·to

NOUN

An issue or situation that is awkward or unpleasant to deal with.
Customer bounced from one person to another.

Here's a hot potato experience you may have had. You're at a restaurant. While eating your meal, you want another drink. You can't find your waiter, so you flag the waiter at the next table and make your request. "I'll tell your server," you're told. And—bounce! Your meal gets cold, and you enjoy your meal less because you have to wait for the waiter whose getting paid to serve you.

Make-mom-proud restaurants choose a teamwork model, where how people are paid doesn't affect service. Their teams pull together because, in the end, fulfilled customers will come back to benefit them all.

Show up as a team to your customer.

This is our opportunity to show up for customers as one company pulling in the same direction to support their needs. But sometimes we lose our customers in the "silo Bermuda triangle." This happens when we get busy doing our individual tasks. When we haven't knit together all of the points that a customer moves through in trying to get something accomplished. And when training, metrics, process, and pay don't unite people as a team. As a result, the customer is bounced across our organization charts. Or passed between our partners and ourselves.

Andrea was so excited to be purchasing her new home. She saved for seven years to get her down payment and to achieve a credit rating that would qualify her for a loan. After doing research, Andrea found a mortgage company that she felt comfortable with. What she didn't realize were the many moving parts between her Realtor, mortgage broker, and escrow company that were all interdependent in making her home purchase and move successful.

With the date for closing provided to her by her broker, Andrea arranged to take a week off work to make her move and settle in. She planned for both movers and her new furniture to be delivered the day after her closing date.

But on the night before her move, she was informed that the required paperwork between her mortgage and escrow companies was not completed, delaying her closing by at least one day, and possibly two. Three required forms between the companies had not been completed. What Andrea *really* needed in this situation is what all customers crave; a close-knit team that worked on her behalf. **Would you pass your mom around like a hot potato?**

Make-mom-proud companies proactively build bridges for customers, both inside their companies and with external partners. They get rid of the "Bermuda Triangle" moments that happen in the handoffs between silos and partners, causing disappointments such as Andrea's.

So, think for a moment, are there any "Bermuda Triangle" moments in your customer journey? Do you unite how people work together, and build bridges across the silos and with partners to deliver a "one company" experience? Do you deliver cross-company accountability to customers, so that no matter whom they encounter in your company, they never experience the "bounce"?

Here's one key action that Wegmans Food Markets takes to build the teamwork that makes them stand out. They invest in fourteen weeks of team building prior to any store opening, making sure that everyone comes together to help each other and customers. By creating a "one-company" experience inside the company and delivering it to customers, Wegmans earns more content employees and happier customers, achieving only 4 percent turnover in their full-time employees—unheard-of in this industry!

A Case Study to #MakeMomProud

Wegmans Food Markets Decided to Train Teams That ACT!

DECISION INTENT: Deliver a "one Wegmans" experience. At Wegmans, their employees who are stocking cans of tuna, working behind the deli counter, or bagging your groceries all pull together to deliver a consistently joyful experience. Wegmans honors employees as a critical extension of their brand, investing in them to give employees knowledge, information, and trust to act as a team, so no customer stands waiting for help or an answer in that grocery store aisle.

"The first question we ask [as we make decisions] is: 'Is this the best thing for the employee?'" says Kevin Stickles, vice president for human resources. "Our employees are our number one asset, period." It's the mantra they live. And while many companies have mantras that are just as convincing, Wegmans puts their money where their mantra is.

ACTION TO #MAKEMOMPROUD: Fourteen weeks of team training for store openings. When Wegmans is ready to open a store, they seek to extend opportunity for store management and positions from within. Then they invest in up to fourteen weeks of training to get everyone on these newly assembled teams ready to act. They invest the time and resources to unite hundreds of people so that when a new store opens, the team has jelled, the experience for the customer has been run through, and everyone is ready to deliver the Wegmans experience.

It is typical for each new full-time employee to travel to another Wegmans store for forty hours of training, often out of their hometown vicinity. This is quite a healthy investment because Wegmans covers mileage and hotel expenses, and also pays the regular wage for employees in training and provides each with a travel per diem. To give you a sense of this investment, it has been reported that Wegmans committed about $2 million to prepare employees for the opening of their store in Charlottesville, Virginia. At a company where more than half of the store managers started working as teenagers wearing that green apron, it's a badge of honor and trust that sets this company apart.

Wegmans Trains for Trust and Teamwork. #MakeMomProud.

IMPACT: Wegmans' turnover is about 17 percent for all employees (including part-time, hourly workers) and as low as 4 percent for full-time employees. They have been named one of *Fortune* magazine's 100 Best Companies to Work For for twenty consecutive years, ranking number two in 2017. It's Wegmans' dedication to employee recruiting and training that drive when the company will expand its market footprint. Despite thousands of requests from states to build stores, they put the brake on market expansion until the right people are ready, available, and in place to deliver the Wegmans experience that fuels their growth.

THE MOM LENS

United Teams of Employees Supporting Customers #MakeMomProud.

Wegmans invests in teamwork, ensuring that everyone pulls together for customers. They never want your mom waiting for someone to get permission to act, nor will they pass her on to someone else for service.

Do Your Customers Ever Feel Like a Hot Potato?

How Do You Breed Teamwork and Trust to Unite People Who Serve?

Fix the Paperwork Rigmarole

Nix that lingo and jargon.
And deliver "understanding" to customers.

This storytelling section is a "twofer" because the paperwork rigmarole includes *two* experiences in our lives as customers: (1) business and industry lingo and jargon; (2) the complexity and burden of paperwork.

Nix the lingo and jargon—and the "jibber jabber."

"IT'S NOT RELATIVITY. HE'S TRYING
TO FIGURE OUT HIS POWER BILL."

My Italian grandma, Ermalinda, was quite a feisty woman.

After my grandpa died, all of the household bills and paperwork fell to her. And once in a while she'd ask me to look over something she'd gotten in the mail. "What's all this jibber jabber!" she'd ask, which, in her broken Italian-English, came out more like "Whatsa alla thisa jibbera jabbera?" We'd spend hours going through her bills, statements, and policies as I translated them for her into plainer English. She always had the same response: "Why didn't they just say *that*?" Good question, Grandma!

Write like you talk, like people do.

Our opportunity is to make communicating in plain and simple language a priority. "Write like you talk," as Lands' End founder Gary Comer coached me a million years ago, when I'd write a piece of copy full of corporate-y words. I was so proud of all my words. But that pride in my words was the wrong starting point.

With clear and simple language, make-mom-proud companies work to say more with fewer, less complex words. This begins by prioritizing what customers need to understand, not the words you want to say. It requires taking a long, hard slog through everything you send to customers. Jump inside your customers' shoes and read through your documents with "customer eyes." Trim the fat on your forms. Take out the lingo (acronyms anyone?). Then rewrite it all in a deliberately clear manner. Write your communications like you'd write a letter to your mother.

So let's make this one simple. First, consider putting all your communications through a tool such as the Flesch-Kincaid readability test. It's a simple online tool that will tell you about the readability of what you are sending out there. It's a great unifier for the organization. And it's a terrific tool that will help you write like you talk: in clear and plain language.

Next, make a list of all of the acronyms that seep into your communication—both written and spoken with customers. Then make a commitment to get rid of the acronym soup. Finally, find all the terminology that means something to you but makes your customers scratch their heads. These terms are actually what create barriers in communication and relationships.

You may be surprised at what you find! Acronyms and lingo are the internal shorthand used inside companies. But they cut humans— our customers—out of the equation. Complex language, or our internal language full of acronyms and terms, creates misunderstanding that erodes value and trust. What you need is "outside in" communication that is crafted to communicate *with* customers, not *at* them. Communication that is easy, and even a joy to read.

Clear language appears more real and human. You trust it more. In its simplicity, there's nowhere to hide. As customers, we simply want clear communications that sound like they're from someone who might live next door. We want to read things we can trust—written by people who tell it to us straight.

Health insurance is an industry where lingo and jargon often get in the way of understanding. For example, if I asked you to define these three words, could you? (1) formulary, (2) adjudication, (3) co-insurance. If you know them, and can use them in a sentence, you may be in the insurance industry. If you don't, and can't, you're like the rest of us, skimming those words, not totally certain of their meaning. That's why Premera Blue Cross, a health insurance company based in Seattle, decided to engage the entire company in an effort called "Let's Be Clear." When a complex industry is trying to make changes, there can be a very long tail from action to customer impact. But communication changes are proven to have an immediate impact, both inside the company and with customers. It's a relief to employees when they are given the opportunity to speak and write in plain language.

Step one for Premera was to identify the top twenty words in health insurance that make customers scratch their heads and go "Huh?" Not a difficult list to compile. Premera immediately began getting rid of those words and replacing them with understandable terms in documents, forms, collateral material, website copy, and language used in the call centers. Some terms couldn't be removed due to legal reasons (insurance is tricky that way), so customers are given a decoder for them when they appear in Premera's communication.

Teams throughout the company pulled together to rewrite both letters and communications with simplified language. But what's made this companywide effort catch fire are the fun "Jargon jars" placed everywhere. When someone's language falls into "insurance speak," and especially those twenty terms, they have to feed the jar. People are challenged: **"Would you use those words with your mom or neighbor?"** All the money collected goes to the United Way. Perhaps the jargon jar is something you may want to try yourself!

Deliver "understanding" to customers. Not more paper.

A LITTLE LIGHT READING TO GO
WITH THAT NEW INSURANCE POLICY.

In 1690, when philosopher John Locke released his famous work
An Essay Concerning Human Understanding, he explained in the
book's introduction why it was so long:

> *I will not deny, but possibly [this] might be reduced to a nar-*
> *rower compass than it is; and that some parts of it might be*
> *contracted: The way it has been writ in, by Catches, and many*
> *long Intervals of Interruption, being apt to cause some Repeti-*
> *tions. But to confess the Truth, I am now too lazy, or too busy*
> *to make it shorter.*

Essentially he's saying that if he'd had more time, he would have
removed some parts, cleaned it up, and simplified it a bit. Certainly
Mr. Locke couldn't have predicted the piles of paper we all receive as

customers, which could do with that same kind of scrubbing and sim-
plification. But he was prophetic in describing the opportunity at
hand!

Every company has paperwork. The more complex the business or
service, the more paper customers receive. Duplicates and triplicates
at times, of the same thing. But in all of that paperwork, "understanding" can go missing for customers. This is the opportunity to make the
paperwork process easier to understand so that customers can know
and value what they will, and will not, receive from you to help them
with their lives.

Let your paperwork navigate customers to clarity and understanding.

Delivering value and understanding means sorting through everything you send to customers with "customer eyes." And as Locke
made a point about above, remove the duplicates sent to customers
and the extra process steps we make them endure.

Let's take that pile of home or automotive insurance documents
you have somewhere at home. Do you know (for sure) what's covered
in yours? According to CNN, a telephone survey conducted for
Trusted Choice, a consumer brand of the Independent Insurance
Agents & Brokers of America, showed alarming results. Nearly 40
percent of respondents don't know what's in their policies. Forty percent also said they weren't confident they have adequate coverage.
That's because the enormity of the pile makes people give up before
digging in. **Would you send your pile of paperwork to your mother?**

Yes, there is paperwork your customers have to send, but you
should strive to decode it and simplify it. Give people a choice on how
to fill it out and more convenience in how to submit it. Reduce the
redundancy, the number, the duplication, and complexity of forms.

You'll stand apart because *that* behavior means you put your customers' lives first. Make the flip from sending paperwork to inform and comply to guiding customers with content, information, and education.

Our next case study is about an action taken by the United Services Automobile Association (USAA). They never consider themselves done with improving how they communicate with members. In fact, they went through a deliberate process to repurpose all communications, to move from "sending documents" to "providing guidance." That is the opportunity that arises every time a pile of paper, or a single letter or tweet, goes out to customers. Here is how they removed a member pain point—and a lot of paperwork rigmarole—to improve the experience of filing a fraudulent credit card claim.

A Case Study to #MakeMomProud

USAA Decided to Simplify the Paper Trail.

DECISION INTENT: Make it easier to report and resolve solve a credit card fraud. USAA's credit card division simplified the typical paperwork trail required to report credit card fraud. It's bad enough when someone somehow got your credit card number and charged things from who-knows-where on your card. Once you get over the panic that your card has been compromised, another one sets in: How do you get those charges reversed? USAA had a fraud resolution process that worked but that was "paperwork rich," you might say. What their process required, as many banks do, was a form that had to be filled out for each and every charge disputed. One of USAA's customers was going through this process to reverse a fraudster's twenty fraudulent charges. So as the process dictated at the time, the customer had to print the form, fill out the form, and scan, fax, or mail the form. Twenty times!

ACTION TO #MAKEMOMPROUD: Peace of mind in one form, and less time. USAA examined that fraud reporting process that burdened their members, and reworked the experience. The rules were changed so that regardless of the number of fraudulent charges made, if they came from one incident, members could now submit one report. They eliminated the laborious process requiring members to print the form, fill it out, scan, fax, or mail it—moving the entire process online. The new system would have saved that member with twenty incidents a ton of time—but his feedback drove the change for the entire system. So, what he lost in time was made up for in his heroism in helping others avoid that paperwork trail.

All USAA actions are grounded in the mission to support the military and their families. Knowing they need easy access to data and information and simple processes leads USAA to constantly rework what they do to get rid of paperwork rigmarole and lengthy processes. They imagine members' lives and change what they can to support them. For example, in 2009, USAA was the first bank to enable remote deposit capture by taking a picture of a check.

USAA Simplifies the Paperwork to Simplify their Member's Lives. #MakeMomProud.

IMPACT: USAA is now a $27 billion, ninety-five-year-old company that continues to innovate on behalf of its customers. For consistently behaving in this manner, USAA earns the renewal of 98 percent of customers each year. And they achieve top ranking of Net Promoter® Scores among all companies from 2009 through the present day. Employees feel working for USAA is a noble cause. They have made *Fortune* Magazine's 100 Best Companies to Work For list for twelve years.

THE MOM LENS

Straight Talk and Clear and Simple Language #MakeMomProud.

In everything that USAA does, they think of their members first: their lives, and how they can make it easier and more joyful to do business with them. They constantly rework what they do to get rid of paperwork rigmarole and lengthy processes.

Would You Send Your Paperwork to Your Mom?

Do You Deliver Understanding Instead of Jargon and Piles of Paper?

Don't Make Me Keep Telling My Story.

Know Me. Please.

"I GOT TIRED OF REPEATING MY INFORMATION,
SO I BOUGHT A PARROT."

Do you remember, in what now seems a million years ago, the hoopla when the Ritz-Carlton hotels began saying "Welcome back" to guests who had stayed at their properties before? At the time, it was the pinnacle of customer service—magical, even. How did they do that?

Today being *known* by the companies who serve us is an expectation. Table stakes. As customers, we expect companies to "know me," "remember me." Yet, after all these years some companies still don't recognize customers, welcome them back, and use their stored memory of each customer to build relationships and bonds, and earn the right to grow.

KNOW ME. PLEASE.

Does it make you a little bit nutty when you're asked to repeat your information and purchases and experiences back to companies who serve you? If yes . . . you're not alone. Accenture found that 89 percent of customers get frustrated because they need to repeat their issues to multiple representatives. Or repeat their stories to retail merchants who simply don't seem to know them.

Accenture also found that 87 percent of customers want brands to put more effort into providing a consistent experience in order to meet their desire to be known across channels. According to PricewaterhouseCoopers, by 2020 the demand for a one-company Omni-Channel customer experience will be amplified by the need for near perfect execution. **Would you make your mom keep reintroducing herself to you?**

With all of us expecting a "You know me" experience, industries that aren't yet delivering it to us feel a little bit behind. And that is the opportunity. The people who know who we are, who record our behaviors and purchases, are those we are gravitating to in our expectation of personalization.

With Netflix, Amazon, and even banks like First Direct keeping our data organized to know us and deliver a relevant "we know you" experience, every company needs to build up to that same capacity for **caring by knowing and delivering relevant, personalized experiences.**

Our case study company, shopping service Stitch Fix, has built their entire business model around "you know me." Chief Executive Katrina Lake's goal was to build a scalable and profitable business serving every woman who desired a personalized wardrobe curating service. They have done a masterful job of blending data science and an understanding of customers' needs and preferences and shopping behavior. They have made "You know me" their growth engine. What makes their model hard to copy is the humanity they have wrapped around delivering relevance that matters to the customer. Theirs is an approach to business growth worth understanding.

A Case Study to #MakeMomProud

Stitch Fix Decided to Make "You Know Me" Their Business Growth Engine.

DECISION INTENT: Personalize and scale "You know me." To scale personal shopping to the masses to deliver the customized experience founder Katrina Lake envisioned, Stitch Fix would need to go well beyond utilizing the artful skills of stylists and their individual databases. They would need to build an engine blending artificial intelligence, data scientists, and stylists to deliver reliable and relevant personal shopping experiences that *feel* relevant and reliable.

ACTION TO #MAKEMOMPROUD: Humanizing the usage of data science. Stitch Fix employs a three-part plan to get "You know me" right. First, they ask for measurements, style likes and dislikes, customer lifestyle, and clothing needs, along with client photos. And they ask for any Pinterest pins the client may have marked. They cleverly use those Pinterest pins in programmed algorithms to help clarify style beyond what someone can fill out on a form. This rare blend of humanity and expertise and data is Stitch Fix's first step to delivering personally curated clothing consistently to masses.

Next, they use data science to deliver a scalable personalized experience. The algorithms that come out of the data provided, overseen by Eric Colson, chief algorithms officer at Stitch Fix, spit out suggestions for stylists to use—everything from sizing to location; geography; body type; and fabric, color, and pattern preferences. These tools are so potent that they can narrow down many options of, for example, pants, to those few that the customer is statistically likely to keep.

Third, Stitch Fix's 3,400 stylists work through the rich content to humanize and personalize the experience. They create customized boxes of five items for each of their clients. As a client's orders increase, the data science improves to deliver more results that are spot-on for customers. Stylists also increase their personalization as they get closer to clients. My friend Mindy, for example, recently requested loose and comfortable clothing in preparation for a surgery. Her stylist sent the customized order, and also a floral bouquet with her best wishes for a speedy recovery.

Eric Colson has said, "Our business is getting relevant things into the hands of our customers.... We couldn't do this with machines alone. We couldn't do this with humans alone. We're just trying to get them to combine their powers."

Stitch Fix Delivers Human Relevant Experiences. #MakeMomProud.

IMPACT: At Amazon, 35 percent of purchases are driven by recommendations. At LinkedIn, it is 50 percent. 100 percent of Stitch Fix purchases are made from recommendations. In less than six years, Stitch Fix has become profitable when other retailers are struggling. Revenue reported to date is $730 million. Stitch Fix has nearly tripled its head count over the past two years and now has 2,800 mostly part-time stylists, many working from home, and more than a thousand warehouse workers across five locations.

THE MOM LENS

Delivering a "You Know Me" Experience #MakesMomProud.

Stitch Fix blends data with humanity and customization. They blend high tech with high touch to deliver personalized "You know me" experiences.

Do Your Customers Feel That You "Know" Them?

Are Gestures and Communications Relevant to Their Relationship with You?

Summarizing
"Don't Make Me Feed You Soap!"

"Bar of soap actions" make customers' lives harder than they have to be. Pure and simple. It's the stuff that you know would make your mom's life harder. The things that you have encountered as a customer that:

* Take up your time.

* Frustrate you (or more) emotionally.

* Give you a brain cramp from being overly complicated.

* Lead to service exhaustion because you have to do the work.

In this chapter, we reflected on the basics that customers would expect from anyone in business. Do you honor customers' time, and their clock? Do you inadvertently layer the work on the customer to do? Are you open and proactive in communication? Are customers honored when they depart? Bounced around? Is reaching you for help a joy or a challenge?

When they exist, "bar of soap" actions interrupt your relationships with customers. If customers experience too many of them, they can send you packing. And "bar of soap" actions quite simply make your employees nuts. Because when your customers are doing the "arm wrestling," your front line is often on the other side of that tussle.

But when reversed, and these moments are eliminated, companies stand out. Customers stop the tussle. Relationships replace transactions. And growth results. Every industry has its own version of "bar of soap" moments. Make-mom-proud companies gladly do the work to find them and get them *o-u-t*!

To put this in the simplest terms, do you deliver pain or pleasure? Do you make it easy and a joy for your customers to do business with you?

TAKE ACTION!

Do you have any "bar of soap" moments
in your customers' experience?

Chapter 6, "Stop the Shenanigans!," will help you evaluate where you are today. It will serve as a mirror test for you to work through with your company and teams. There you will find each of the opportunities and studies to #MakeMomProud outlined with questions to plot your current state. Your evaluation will help you to plan your actions to nudge your company along to where you want it to be.

Please also go to customerbliss.com, where you can download training videos for these stories, the comics, and a leader guide so you can use this material inside your company.

4.

Put Others Before Yourself.

To reach your goals, help others to achieve theirs.

"We make a living by what we get.
We make a life by what we give."
—WINSTON CHURCHILL

Like our moms, the make-mom-proud companies prove with their actions that they have their customers' best interests in mind. This is at the heart of companies that grow most organically—earning ardent admirers who grow their business for them. They earn a bigger piece of the pie because they improve customers' lives.

This is a simple idea to accept, but oh so hard to execute. Operating at this level remains elusive until the paradoxical realization kicks in: **To achieve your goals, you need to help others achieve theirs.**

To take this approach to growth means opening everyone up to a new order of design and decision making. In practical terms, this means building a "peace of mind" experience for travel customers to ensure they reach their destination, or crafting a welcome experience to your services. It's about building deliberate moments of trust based on customer needs and delivering memories earned by serving lives.

This goes well beyond "whack-a-moling" problems away—to imagining the people and the emotions and the lives that you serve.

Ask yourself: What's the foundation of your business? What drives your organization to action? At the root of make-mom-proud companies that take this outside-in approach are the lives of the people at the end of their decisions. When these companies think about how to improve their products and experiences, they imagine the emotions of their customers, and the goals their customers want to achieve. They grow by designing products, solutions, and experiences for life's real moments.

At Cole Haan's innovation center, for example, they imagine your life in shoes. Designers and innovators obsess about what you *do* throughout your day, your week, and your year, in every kind of shoe. They literally endeavor to walk in their customers' shoes. Where and when, for example, do women start feeling the pinch of those high heels? Scott Patt, Cole Haan's vice president of design and innovation, summed it up like this for *Fast Company*: "The work we do here is driven by the belief that the work we are doing can improve people's lives."

This "imagining" of people's lives was how we grew the business many years ago at Lands' End, where I found a home early in my career. We imagined the UPS driver handing a mom a package with the first pair of overalls for her child. We thought about how those overalls needed to have reinforced knees so she wouldn't need to keep replacing them.

When we started making swimsuits for women, we began with the emotion (oh, the emotion!) of swimsuit shopping and looking at ourselves in the mirror, tugging and pulling. We asked our best customers if they would partner with us to build a better suit. And ended up flying in hundreds of women to Dodgeville, Wisconsin, to join us at the big Olympic pool in the Lands' End activity center. There we watched them get in and out of the pool and swim laps. Where they yanked, we changed, and where they pulled, we fixed.

We looked back on our lives as kids playing with the shipping boxes as much as the toys—and got inspired to print the head and tail of a cow, a sheep or a horse on the flaps—so kids could ride their Lands' End box all over the house! More than thirty years later, people still tell me about those boxes. We started with the life. We yearned to deserve customer love. We started there and worked for it.

Designing experiences and products from the customers' point of view is a virtuous way to grow. And it takes leadership and commitment and unity to challenge the status quo and rebuild from the outside in.

Human-centered and customer-centered design means flipping the leadership and operational mind-set from designing for what you want to *get* from customers, to designing what you want to give customers, so they can achieve their goals. So they can see and feel value.

Designing operations, processes, products, and services to improve customers' lives requires a shift in the origin of design: from internal, company-driven priorities and focus, to external customer emotions, priorities, and needs. When customers achieve their goals *because of their association with you*, they will reward you with advocacy and growth. And they will share how you helped them achieve their goals, becoming a volunteer army to help you grow your business.

Necessity *may be* the mother of invention, but mothers are an inspiration to virtuous business growth. Their no-strings-attached treatment reminds us of what pulls us toward people who have our best interests at heart.

Our opportunity to become this kind of company is to design for no-strings-attached life improvements. It is this expansion of moving past what is required to what is desired that changes and elevates companies.

What this chapter holds for you are reinventions, transformations, and disruptions that have grown companies and drawn employees and customers closer. Some are big, some small. What matters in all of these stories is their starting place. They all begin with the lives, emotions, and needs of customers as the inspiration for design or the impetus of change.

The make-mom-proud companies here all prove that they've achieved their goals by paving the way for their customers to achieve theirs.

Have Clarity of Purpose.

Unite the company on how you improve lives.

Airbnb, the online marketplace and hospitality service that's become emblematic of the sharing economy, decided they needed to redefine their purpose in 2013. They began asking, "Why does Airbnb exist? What's its purpose? What's its role in the world?" What they discovered is that hosts and guests alike desired to have a sense of *belonging*. They were interested in landing in and nestling into new places. They sought to experience and see sides of a city authentically, not as a tourist. To live as locals do, even for a little while.

Since then, Airbnb has existed to create a global culture of *belonging*: they work to enable people to "belong anywhere." This takes the company beyond helping customers find a cool place to stay at a great price; their purpose is higher. "Belong anywhere" simultaneously steers business operations toward a human and personal guest experience that feels like home; it unites employees in experience innovation, and it guides Airbnb in achieving its higher purpose to help people "belong anywhere" in the world. This shift has given Airbnb the solid foundation to continue its growth trajectory and marketplace differentiation.

Make-mom-proud companies make it their priority to clarify their purpose. **Clarity of purpose gives people's work meaning.** It's the glue that unites a team and enables everyone to look beyond their individual tasks so they can deliver a one-company experience that customers want to have again.

Clarity of purpose unites behaviors and actions inside an organization to deliver meaningful experiences. Call center reps are considered critical to delivering customer value and rescuing customers in pain. Retail folks on the floor are hired and developed to guide their customers to a moment of retail therapy joy. Deliverymen and women are part of the bigger picture of delivering peace of mind.

Let your purpose unite your company.

The make-mom-proud companies put in the work to clarify *why* they exist. Then they do the heavy lifting to embed that purpose into the way they behave and operate the business. They link their purpose with whom they hire, how they conduct themselves, and what they will and will not do to grow. Clarity of purpose is their foundation for company behavior and growth.

Gerber has thrived for ninety years because their mission is being parents' trusted partner, supporting parenthood, and taking the mystery out of what they call "mom life." They focus not only on the products they sell, but also on being part of people's lives, offering

information, community, and nurturing guidance to families throughout their many years in business.

When your company has clarity of purpose, everyone can define
your unique promise for customers' lives—and take it to heart. Your
purpose guides individual and team choices—connecting work across
the organization. It elevates people's work from executing tasks to
delivering experiences customers want to repeat and tell others about.

The make-mom-proud companies have done the hard work to
clarify why they exist and whom they serve. IKEA, which we explore
in detail in the case study, built its business from a foundation of creating solutions "for the many" who want to create a comfortable home.

Zappos is grounded as a service company that happens to sell
shoes. DaVita, one of the leading kidney-care companies in the
United States, has made their purpose "giving life." DaVita "moments
of heroism" recognize and reinforce actions and behaviors that align
with that purpose. "Giving life" unites the operation, and provides a
lens for decision making and action. And the DaVita operating model,
inspired by their purpose, is an integrated approach to keeping
kidney-care patients healthy.

Connect everyone's work
to how you improve lives.

Clarity of purpose unleashes an organization's imagination to
make decisions guided by its promise. It's no wonder that companies
with clarity of purpose have the most loyal and engaged employees.
The opportunity to deliver a purpose consistently understood and
expected elevates day-to-day tasks to part of achieving a higher purpose, giving work direction and joy.

According to the 2017 *Grant Thornton International Business*

Report, 70.5 percent of dynamic—or high-growth—companies across the world have a clearly defined nonfinancial purpose. And people are taking note of what companies stand for, and making buying decisions armed with that information. GlobeScan research shows that 40 percent of the world's emerging middle class "seeks brands that have a clear purpose, and act in the best interests of society."

So who are you? **Is your company united in how you improve customers' lives?** How would your greatest accomplishments as a company be described—based on "why" you are in business? At the end of each day, month, or year, how do you measure success?

Here, as promised, is more detail than you might ever have known about how IKEA came to be, and the "why" behind its promise that has fueled its growth.

A Case Study to #MakeMomProud

IKEA Decided to "Create a better everyday life for the many people."

DECISION INTENT: Be there for the many people. IKEA knows its purpose. Its ability to consistently live it fuels its growth. Its purpose is to be there for its customers when they have more sweat equity than money in their pockets. IKEA makes you put together your own furniture, herd salespeople to get help, and bring your goods to your car. But this is all for good reason: so that the many can feather their nests, and build a place to call home at a good value. This is a commitment that IKEA has unwaveringly stayed true to since 1943, when the late Ingvar Kamprad, who was only seventeen years old at the time, started IKEA.

ACTION TO #MAKEMOMPROUD: Provides customers low price with *meaning*. IKEA's identity is low price with a *meaning*—with quality and functionality that must always adapt to serve customers' needs. In his 1975 manifesto *The Testament of a Furniture Dealer*, Kamprad said, "*[Our purpose is] to create a better everyday life for the many people by offering a wide range of well-designed, functional home furnishing products at prices so low that as many people as possible will be able to afford them.*"

Kamprad connects the purpose of low price with a meaning to everyone in the organization: "*That includes product developers, designers, buyers, office and warehouse staff, salespeople and all other cost bearers who are in a position to influence our purchase prices and all our other costs—in short, every single one of us! Without low costs, we can never accomplish our purpose.*"

This clarity continues to drive IKEA's global expansion today. It is driven to design the price tag first, starting with the "lives of the many people" who, for example, need a chair for their living room. It's what drives giving customers the pieces of that chair in a box to put together themselves. It drives what IKEA calls the "human resource" promise to find and nurture "down-to-earth, straight-forward people," both as individuals and in their professional roles. It drives why it sells those Swedish meatballs, as both a nod to Kamprad and IKEA's origins and also that it is *good value for the money*—the ultimate test that everything and everyone must live up to.

IKEA creates a better everyday life for many. #MakeMomProud.

IMPACT: Considered the largest furniture retailer in the world, *Forbes* ranks IKEA's brand as the forty-first most valuable brand in the world, growing to 393 stores in forty-eight countries, welcoming more than 545 million visitors worldwide. In 2016, IKEA was named one of *Fortune's* 100 Best Companies to Work For. Its focus and clarity has established fans who gravitate to the "IKEA effect," which is about pride in value, economy, and doing things oneself.

THE MOM LENS

Living Your Purpose and Promise #MakesMomProud.

IKEA lives its purpose of "being there for the many people." It unites every silo, every person, and every operation to deliver value to customers at the times in their lives when it's needed.

Do You Have Clarity of Purpose?

Is Everyone Connected in Improving Customers' Lives?

Start with Life, Not the Action Item.

Honor the human right in front of you.

"PLEASE FILL OUT THESE FORMS FIRST."

How we're greeted as customers tells us a lot about the treatment we're about to receive. Whether you're placing a call to a company, checking in at a hotel, walking into a retailer, or visiting the doctor, that first moment of contact cements it. And as you're standing there, or still in the line waiting, you get that little catch in your throat while waiting to be acknowledged.

Beth feels fortunate because under her employer's health-care plan, she can go to an urgent-care clinic in town along with her family members for no additional co-pay. As a teacher on a limited income, this puts her mind at ease. But every time she checks in at the front desk, it feels like filling out forms is the main priority of the front desk personnel. When she gets a "hello," it's from someone behind the desk who lifts his head momentarily from his computer screen. What Beth really wants is what we all want: to be *the* priority—she wants those employees to acknowledge her with respect and ask how they can help her.

What we all yearn for is to be recognized and welcomed. And to have our priorities understood and acted upon. How you welcome customers gives them important clues about what the rest of their experience will be like. It's all too easy to slip into an ultra-efficient routine that inadvertently focuses on internal processes rather than the human right in front of you.

Would you invite your mom to an event at your home, **then give her a number and ask her to take a seat?** Of course not. You'd welcome her in, ask how she was doing, and make her comfortable. You'd make sure she knew you acknowledged her importance.

Honor the human right in front of you.

Make-mom-proud companies act on people's desire to be acknowledged. Hyatt Hotels, which we mentioned earlier, focused their human-centered redesign on the "moment of recognition" we need with a check-in experience. CEO Mark Hoplamazian said that this work began when he personally observed Hyatt's check-in experience from the perspective of the human customer, rather than from the hotel chain's. As a result, Hyatt spent two years developing a system that redirects the front desk clerk's initial focus from keying in the reservation to greeting and welcoming the customer. The redesign has led to an increased focus on hiring personal and engaged people at that front counter. Now empathy and a human connection, rather than the sound of those clicking keys, are hallmarks of a Hyatt hotel welcome.

The great opportunity here is to redesign your welcome—to rethink your "hello" with welcoming eye contact and by calling customers by name. This all sounds intuitive—of course we should warmly and personally greet our customers. But the truth is that this is the exception rather than the rule: ContactPoint client research has found that on average, employees ask or welcome customers by name only 21 percent of the time.

Be the company that always honors the person first. Before you do anything else, acknowledge the customer reaching out to you. Care genuinely. Know his or her name. This small acknowledgment paves the way for real relationships that go beyond transactions. It sets make-mom-proud companies apart, and it won't cost a thing. Humanity trumps paperwork.

Here is how Canada's Mayfair Diagnostics in Calgary, Alberta, completely redesigned the check-in experience at their imaging centers—by understanding the emotional responses people have to the front desk, to eye contact, and to how they are either "processed" or cared for. I hope you will be inspired by their human-centered redesign and the results achieved when they rethought their "hello."

A Case Study to #MakeMomProud

Mayfair Diagnostics Decided on a Human-Centered Welcome.

DECISION INTENT: Deliver a nurturing welcome. When a doctor writes an order for any type of diagnostic test, such as imaging, worry, fear, and concern invade our thoughts until the test is done and the results are in. This is because paperwork and procedure often define this experience. As patients, we can feel like one of many files of paperwork being processed and queued and ultimately told our results. Yet we always hope for more. A little more urgency, a little more empathy, and a little more care can help us grapple with what is happening to us for the procedure.

Mayfair Diagnostics in Calgary, Alberta, chose to rethink and redesign this emotional journey for the more than seven hundred thousand patients it serves each year. They sought to have a more deliberate role in supporting and serving; standing out as a service organization, and earning the right to grow through experience, empathy, and giving patients and their families clarity and control.

ACTION TO #MAKEMOMPROUD: A redesigned welcome. Mayfair learned that most patients entering their clinic have an emotional need to "be received." But the traditional clinic process is that patients are "checked in." Arrival? Check. Insurance? Check. Paperwork? Check. "Have a seat. We'll call your name." In contrast, in the new Mayfair experience, patients are contacted prior to their visit by a clinic host who prepares them and gets to know them. Then when they arrive, they are welcomed and received by staff who go beyond the paper-

work to understand any special needs and get patients and their families situated.

Understanding people's emotions led Mayfair to reconfigure several key areas that affect patients' well-being, and how they felt they were being cared for and welcomed. Key among these insights, which became a foundation for design, is the importance of eye contact. They learned that when patients stand in front of a counter looking down, it creates an imbalanced relationship between the customer and the company. So the new welcome experience at the Mayfair Clinics is wrapped around a "welcome pod." Hosts greet patients standing at the welcome pod, where he or she can make eye contact and connect. And then, just as we learned from Nordstrom and the Four Seasons, they then walk around from behind the pod to welcome and support their guests. "Designing empathy into the patient experience requires a fundamental shift in organizational operation and mind-set," Jackie McAtee, who oversaw the transformation, told me. "Simply adding a few iPads to the waiting room won't accomplish this change."

Mayfair begins with the patient, not the paperwork. #MakeMomProud

IMPACT: This new redesigned clinic became profitable three months ahead of schedule. The initial Net Promoter Score for the clinic was three points above the company average. Patient feedback has been overwhelmingly positive, with requests and pleas to have service done at this new clinic.

THE MOM LENS

A Warm, Genuine, and Caring "Hello" #MakesMomProud.

Mayfair Diagnostics redesigned the welcome experience by looking into the eyes of the patients who walk through their door, and guiding—never "processing"—the humans standing in front of them.

> ## Does Your "Hello" Focus on People or Process?
>
> *Are We Honoring Customers with Our Welcome? Always?*

Allow for Human Error.
Design in Empathy and Care.

To earn your place, offer grace.

SCREECH!

"THREE SECONDS LATE.
THAT'S ANOTHER DAY'S RENTAL CHARGE!"

In Uganda, women entrepreneurs often experience a vicious no-win cycle. Often limited to loans with very high rates, short cycles for repayment, and late fee penalties, no matter how hard they work, it's very difficult for them to get ahead. Understanding and empathizing with their plight, the Uganda Women Entrepreneurship Programme began giving qualifying women extended grace periods for loan repayment and improved loan terms. Benefits are given, based on how long each has generated an income for their business. Giving these women a chance to get ahead, this Programme designs in empathy and care, allowing qualifying women to repay their loans interest free for the first twelve months.

When we are in vulnerable positions, like the Ugandian women entrepreneurs, we need understanding of our situation and support. We seek a human response grounded in an understanding of what we are going through. Make-mom-proud companies take the time to know the vulnerable times in their customers' lives. With that knowledge, they *design in* warm and caring responses to show up for customers, with empathy and care. These actions are planned as gestures consistently carried out by the company and its people. It's how they weave humanity into their operating model.

For example, when Mercedes Benz learns that a lessee of one of their vehicles has died, the family receives communication from them that says, "We know this is a tough time. We want to help." Bereaved family members receive a condolence letter and a leather journal and pen to help record all of the tasks ahead. And then they offer grace: Mercedes offers families a ten-day time period to return the vehicle, in which all fees are suspended. Alternatively, the family can continue the lease, transferring it to a qualifying family member. Mercedes waives all transfer fees.

To earn your place, offer grace.

This is our opportunity to build empathetic actions into our operating model; to wire in acts of kindness and humanity; and to be inspired to build products and services that help customers in times of need.

Every company and industry can be inspired to deliver in these moments. For example, Wholesome Wave was inspired through the recognition that people on strict budgets can't afford fruits and vegetables. To assist this vulnerable group, they created a national network to enable doctors to write "fruit and vegetable prescriptions" for them. More than 1,400 farmers, markets, and grocery stores are partners in this effort, who redeem their "produce prescriptions." This gesture is helping these folks live a healthier life, reducing their risk of diet-related diseases such as obesity, hypertension, or type-2 diabetes.

What are the moments when your customer is vulnerable? Can you identify the opportunities across your customer journey where you can stand out by stepping up? When can you offer an extension of what your company stands for by operating differently?

Our next case study is about Warby Parker, a business that was inspired, as many of the make-mom-proud companies are, by a desire to do business differently. And that difference was to offer good glasses at a reasonable price—to provide an alternative from an industry dominated by very few manufacturers dictating quality and pricing.

The founders describe how one of them lost his glasses on a backpacking trip, and rather than spend big for a replacement pair, he squinted his way through his first semester of grad school. Who among us hasn't forgone something we need at one time or another because of cost? These four guys started this company because they believe that "everyone has the right to see." And they believe glasses should not feel like a chore—but easy and even fun. Here's how Warby Parker earns their place by offering grace.

A Case Study to #MakeMomProud

Warby Parker Decided on a Thirty-Day "No Questions Asked" Return Policy.

DECISION INTENT: Give customers a grace period. When was the last time a company said to you, "Hey, wear this thing we just sold you. And if you don't like what we sent you—send it back on us." Probably not very frequently. But this happens at Warby Parker because they know stuff happens. And they want to have your back in this moment—when you just sat on your glasses.

ACTION TO #MAKEMOMPROUD: Trusts customers and makes them whole. Many times, when an offer of this nature is extended, rules and guidelines keep it in check to make sure that the customer is not taking advantage. These types of checks and balances are put in place when companies are concerned that customers won't do the right thing. And this is why companies end up creating the majority of their rules: to protect themselves from the minority of their customers.

But when the intention is in the right place, the checks and balances for rule following are not necessary. Even under circumstances that have been documented by zealot customers whose glasses were broken when they stepped on them or dropped them within those thirty days, there are no questions asked; they're replaced. And Warby Parker believes you. Before they receive what's left of your old glasses, new ones are on the way.

The first ground rule at Warby Parker is "Treat customers the way you'd want to be treated." When you call them with those crumpled-up glasses in your hand, or for any other reason, a human being answers your call within six seconds. They are a company of people with common values and a series of rituals that fuse them together (each employee receives a copy of Jack Kerouac's *The Dharma Bums*, whose early characters were named Warby Pepper and Zagg Parker). As a result, you're always greeted with someone happy to work with *you*—because *they* work for a company that lets them take selfless actions that extend grace: actions that help them to grow their business. To make Mom proud, they donate a pair of glasses to someone in need for every pair they sell.

Warby Parker Trusts You. #MakeMomProud.

IMPACT: Through a culture and operation built on value, trust, and personality, the number one driver of sales for Warby Parker is word of mouth. Their Net Promoter Score is near 84, eclipsing other optical retailers performing in single digits. They have grown to an estimated valuation exceeding $1.2 billion. U.S. sales are projected to increase 20 percent in 2017, on top of a 28 percent growth in 2016, according to the market research firm 1010data. When other retailers are closing stores, they are opening them.

THE MOM LENS

Allowing for Human Error and Wiring in Empathy #MakesMomProud.

Warby Parker prospers by letting employees extend grace. They wire in the benefit of the doubt by offering returns for thirty days *no matter what*, trusting customers to do the right thing.

Do You Allow for Human Error?

Where Are You Giving Customers the Benefit of the Doubt?

Earn a Place in the Story of Customers' Lives.

Make memory creation the currency of your brand.

"CONGRATULATIONS ON YOUR NEW HOME! UM...I CAN'T SEE PAST THE PAPERS. IS THERE SOMEONE ELSE IN HERE?"

"Bread, that this house may never know hunger.
"Salt, that life may always have flavor.
"And wine, that joy and prosperity may reign forever."

In the movie *It's a Wonderful Life*, George Bailey and his wife, Mary, as purveyors of the Bedford Falls savings and loan, create a memory for the Martini family as they take possession of their new home. Focusing on celebrating the new life of this family, George Bailey gives his iconic toast: a loaf of bread, a box of salt and a bottle of wine create a memory. George and Mary Bailey became a part of the story of the Martinis' lives.

And if the Martinis were real people and not actors, they would forget about the paperwork and the move as time passed. All of the hassle of the experience would fall away, and instead they would remember their joy, and how the Baileys' took care of them and made them feel.

What Memories Will You Deliver?

This is our opportunity: to craft experiences that earn their place—as positive memories in customers' lives.

Would you celebrate your mom's birthday with a check, but not a call or a hug? By sending her a check you assure her that you remembered her birthday. You meet the expectation of acknowledgment—but miss the opportunity for emotion and memory. Companies miss that nuance sometimes. Execution without customer connection is adequate, but a missed opportunity to give customers remembrance of the moment.

Our opportunity, like that moment with Mom, is to wrap our humanity around the interactions we have with customers. THAT is what will set you apart. Gallup research validates that these moments to connect our experience with customer memory is a major opportunity to create lasting bonds with customers.

Memory creation is, in fact, a choice. In every interaction with customers, you can choose how you'll deliver a memory. The great news is that often that choice comes at no cost. All it requires is that people act on the power they have to deliver a memory. A warm and compassionate call or tweet, how a bag is handed to someone as a sale is ended, even the sound and tone of how information is delivered can make someone's day and deliver a customer's recollection of warmth and compassion.

When you focus on your operation and people on memory creation, not just executing tasks, customers will remember you. And with those memories come the opportunity to earn the right to business growth. For example, from the Bailey mortgage experience, would you be more likely to carry your banking business to a company that really helped and cared for you through one of the biggest purchases of your lives? What if they also delivered a "George Bailey moment" as you took possession of your home?

This next story celebrates how deliberate actions can affect people for their entire lives. The Girl Scouts of Greater New York found a way to dedicate the resources, the time, and the people to create and sustain a special troop for homeless girls. They are now endeavoring to expand this specially created troop throughout all the boroughs of New York to deliver young girls guidance, support, and memories they'll have with them all their lives.

Here is the opportunity we have in our work: Through deliberate actions starting with customers' needs, we can become a part of their lives. What do you do to improve customers' lives and leave a lasting memory?

A Case Study to #MakeMomProud

Girl Scouts of Greater New York Decided to Give Homeless Girls a Troop.

DECISION INTENT: Give homeless girls a place to belong and develop. The Girl Scouts of Greater New York, whose mission is to "build girls of courage, confidence and character who make the world a better place," decided to offer the benefits of scouting to a group previously not served: girls living in shelters. They wanted to find a way to fund and enable scouting for these girls, not only for the lifelong memories and skills that scouting develops, but also for the gifts it could offer them: the stability of a weekly meeting, adults who cared for their well-being, and becoming part of a community of girls with common interests and living circumstances.

ACTION TO #MAKEMOMPROUD: Create Troop 6000 for homeless girls. Through a partnership between the Girl Scouts of Greater New York and the New York City Department of Homeless Services, Troop 6000 was created to give girls living in shelters a sense of self, purpose, and belonging. Now, the members of the troop meet every Friday at the Sleep Inn Motel in Queens, which has been converted to a homeless shelter by the city to accommodate an estimated one hundred homeless families. In their meetings, they take the Girl Scout oath. They work on getting badges and learning skills. They get a sense of stability and see the possibilities available to them beyond their current situation.

Each girl's membership fee and monthly dues are funded by the Girl Scouts of Greater New York. And like every other scout, each receives a starter kit of patches, pins, a manual, and vests. With plans to expand through every borough in New York, this troop will have the designation "Troop 6000" to indicate that it is for this very special set of girls. Their mission: *"Every girl in the five boroughs of New York City deserves a chance to reach her full potential: to have her eyes opened to possibilities for college and careers, to make loving and supportive friends, to learn from caring female mentors, and to chart her own course to achieve her goals."*

Girl Scouts of Greater New York Welcomes Homeless Girls. #MakeMomProud.

IMPACT: Today, there are 2.6 million Girl Scouts—1.8 million girl members and 800,000 adult members working primarily as volunteers to help girls find their place and their path. This effort gives homeless girls in New York a sense of place and home. Like all efforts that begin with the customer, or in this case, these deserving girls, selfless actions deliver positive memories. They earn a place in the story of their lives. Meridith Maskara, chief operating officer of the Girl Scouts of Greater New York, has stated that scouting membership has been transformative for these girls. It has changed their lives.

THE MOM LENS

Taking Genuine Actions to Improve Lives #MakesMomProud.

The Girl Scouts of Greater New York selflessly found a way to fund and support the scouting experience for homeless New York City girls, which they will benefit from and carry with them for the rest of their lives.

> ## Have You Earned a Place in Customers' Lives?
>
> *Are You Fundamentally Adding Value, Beyond Executing Tactics and Actions?*

Design with Emotions in Mind.

Build bonds with emotion-driven innovation.

"I'M USED TO THIS. I'M A PLUMBER."

Ah, the hospital gown. Is there any other piece of clothing that renders us so vulnerable? The minute we slip it on, we feel less like ourselves. Even at a simple doctor's visit, that gown makes us feel cold and uneasy.

Often what sets apart the companies we love is their obsession over how customers feel in certain situations. They work at understanding emotions that are native to customer experiences, such as wearing a gown at a hospital visit. Then they use that understanding to redesign experiences to deliver an outcome that flips the negative emotion to a positive one. For example, in the case of the hospital gown, they turn patient vulnerability into comfort. Emotional understanding of customer experiences is often what leads these companies to their most innovative business practices.

Practice emotion-driven innovation.

Make-mom-proud companies strive for emotion-driven innovation. Through taking the time to understand customer emotions, they transcend transactional relationships and are able to develop products and services that deliberately move customers from concern to control, worry to calm, fear to peace of mind, from helplessness to feeling supported. Innovative practices emerge—by thinking of customers' emotions first.

Here are just a few examples of companies committed to creating remarkable experiences, inspired by human emotion: "Zappos Adaptive" was designed around the emotions of their customers with physical disabilities. Through this initiative, Zappos fulfills its mission of creating footwear that causes feelings of self-sufficiency and pride for their customers.

Cleveland Clinic used their understanding of the stress, worry, and anxiety of parents with infants in their neonatal intensive care unit (NICU) to innovate the practice of installing cameras in the NICUs of their hospitals. Placed over each baby's bed, their "NicView" calms those stressful emotions, and brings joy to new parents. Similarly, the Mayo Clinic knows medical equipment is sometimes scary looking for kids, so they hide cardiopulmonary resuscitation (CPR) equipment behind pictures in children's exam and hospital rooms.

Finally, restaurateur Danny Meyer knows that tipping stirs up emotions—some bad, some good—among both restaurant patrons and restaurant team members, so he eliminated tips so people can focus on the food and the service.

Not surprisingly, these practices are yielding results. Both the Disney Institute and Gallup research tell us that companies that practice emotion-driven innovation earn customer advocates who are three times more likely to recommend them. They are also immune from the competition. And with all of this comes greater sales growth—up to 85 percent higher than competitors who have not engaged emotionally with customers.

This is our opportunity to understand the emotions that come along with customers' journeys with us. Once we understand how our customers feel, we can devote our energy to designing out fear, frustration, worry, and concern.

Is there anything you'd redesign in your company for your mom? Do you know what emotions drive your customers to you, and the emotions that stir in their relationship with you? Do you stew over them and redesign experiences to address and support them?

This next case study is about sick teenagers and that hospital gown that robs them of their personality. Read below to learn how changing this one emotionally charged dimension of their hospital stay brings joy, dignity, and identity for sick teens.

A Case Study to #MakeMomProud

Starlight Children's Foundation Decided to Give Sick Teens Back Their Identity.

DECISION INTENT: Give hospitalized teens dignity and identity. That hospital gown is pretty unpleasant for any of us to slip on. But for sick teens stuck in the hospital, that gown robs them of their identity, and is one more reminder of the life they're not having with their friends. The Starlight Children's Foundation Canada and the ad agency Rethink Canada wanted to give teens a way to express their individuality—and express a little rebellion against that standard-issue robe. They decided it wasn't fair to rob teens of what makes them unique by having to wear a vanilla hospital gown.

In fact, the entire health-care industry is recognizing the importance of that gown to patient dignity. The *Journal of the American Medical Association* suggests patients wearing personalized clothing are more likely to "maintain their self-esteem and orientation, and also remind their care professionals to recognize them as people."

ACTION TO #MAKEMOMPROUD: The WARD + ROBES initiative. The Ward + Robes initiative engaged Canadian artists whose graphics are appealing to teens to create "robes" with patterns and details to fit their style. Teens can now choose from gowns inspired by street wear, meditation mandalas, stylized drawings, and other graphics and adornments that appeal to them. The key is that they pick the gown that fits their style and who they are as a person.

Even the tags on the robes appeal to the teens:

> **You're unique—
> why should your hospital gown
> be any different?**

One of the teen beneficiaries of the new gowns described it this way: *"When you can't wear what you want, you feel like you're not who you should be, or you're just your illness or you're just . . . a hospital patient."* *"Makes me feel like my identity has been stripped from me."* Starlight is seeking to extend the program across Canada, the United States, and beyond. They are raising the spirit of sick teens who previously felt their identity was lost in that robe.

Ward + Robes Gives Sick Teens Their Identity Back. #MakeMomProud.

IMPACT: The impact of this initiative is in the emotional transformation of these kids the minute they slip on their newly designed robe. I'll let the words of the teens in the Starlight Children's Foundation videos speak for themselves on the impact they have had on their emotional well-being and their lives. *"This gown lets me be who I am outside of the hospital, and outside of being ill. I feel like I'm myself—it doesn't feel like I'm in a hospital anymore."* *"When I first saw the new gowns, I saw empowerment in teenagers—in a place where they don't have any. I feel like I'm supposed to feel in it."*

THE MOM LENS

Designing Out Negative or Vulnerable Emotions #MakesMomProud.

By understanding the importance of individuality to sick teens, the Starlight Children's Foundation gives a little bit of their identity back with hospital gowns that let them express themselves.

Do You Understand Your Customer's Emotions?

Are Experiences Designed to Earn Positive Emotional Responses?

Walk Customers Out of Trouble Spots.

Invest in "being there."

"WE MISSED YOUR CONNECTION. BUT SEE,
I TOLD YOU I WOULD GET YOU ON THIS FLIGHT."

Tony was on the fourth leg of his business trip when a mechanical error delayed his outbound flight and caused him to miss his connection. A long-term and valuable member of his airline's loyalty plan, he figured "they've got me here." He was relieved when the first text came that said that the airline knew his connection had departed without him, and they were working on another flight. A second text offered the next available flight on the airline four hours later.

If he took the flight his airline proposed, Tony would miss his meeting and dinner. So, Tony started scrambling and searching, and found a partner airline flight departing the airport in 1.5 hours, with seats available. The price was about the same as his ticket. He would make his meeting! But the customer service agent said that they couldn't transfer his ticket over. He heard something about the partner holding the seats as he hung up the phone and started running . . .

Increasingly stressed over missing his meeting, Tony ran to the gate of the partner airline, doled out the cash for a new ticket, and made the earlier flight. He had to fend for himself. He had to do what he thought the airline would be able to do for him, as one of their most valued customers.

There's nothing like that panic that builds inside of us when we know our options are diminishing. We hate feeling alone at those times, and hate being left to our own devices to figure it out. **Would you let Mom fend for herself? Or would you rescue her?**

Invest in "being there."

This is our opportunity to give our customers the sense that we "have them" in moments when they could use a little help. Make-mom-proud companies have their customers' backs because they obsess about knowing when to rescue customers—or reach out with a kind helping hand. They create customer plans ready to be acted upon when needed . . . or when they want to show up like no other company in their customers' life.

Patagonia's "Worn Wear College Tour," for example, travels to college campuses around the United States to repair students' clothing free of charge, and to teach students to fix their own clothes. And they'll do this for any brand in students' closets—not just their own. Patagonia strives to "be there" for students—in that time in their lives when they need to get every mile they can out of that pair of jeans or shirt. Is this something these students knew that they needed? They wouldn't have said so if you'd asked them in a survey.

Make-mom-proud companies create a bond with customers because they are there *even when people didn't know they needed them,* just like Mom. Are you there for customers?

Think of all of the ways you can let your customers know you're thinking of them. Plan how you'll rescue them in moments of hardship. But also plan inspired experiences, just like Patagonia's—that customers won't want to live without. It will bond you to them.

Our next case study has at its heart smoothing out the bumpy road of our travel experiences and giving every employee the ability to make someone's day, on the spot, no permission required. Alaska Airlines 'empowerment toolkit lets *every* employee act when they see a frantic customer like Tony. Or when they see a moment for celebration. I know you'll enjoy their story.

A Case Study to #MakeMomProud

Alaska Airlines Decided That Employees Can Make It Right.

DECISION INTENT: Trust employees to care for customers on the spot. *Everyone* at Alaska Airlines is held accountable, given permission, and trusted to help a customer in need. Ben Minicucci, Alaska's president and COO, gives employees permission to act at work like they'd act at home: "Do what you think is right," he tells employees. "We trust you. You'll never get in trouble for making a decision. **And we don't want you to call the supervisor.**"

ACTION TO #MAKEMOMPROUD: "We Trust You" empowerment toolkit. Alaska Airlines, like other make-mom-proud companies, takes the long view in investing in hiring the right people with service in their personal DNA, and then enabling them to act. They train and then trust. Everyone hired, including baggage handlers, the people at departures, gate agents, flight crew, service reps at the airport, and those on the phone, are prepared for the vulnerable moments when humanity means the most to a traveler in distress. The airline travel experience is fraught with potential opportunities for customer frustration and disappointment—and this is when connecting and showing up as human is most critical.

"Connect first, then decide how to act" is the approach employees are guided to take. Each is encouraged to "find the story of the customer, and create a personal connection." That informs how they decide to act and personalize solving a challenging customer experience, such as a delayed or canceled flight. Based on loose guidelines, people are trusted to extend miles, money, restaurant vouchers, and fee waivers—some of the gestures proactively given to them to use—without asking anyone. Customer service agents receive special training in how to humanly help, and they have more options in addition to their tool kit gestures that they are free to act upon. Mobile devices give reps updates on customer situations and tools to help them. For example, when customers agree to be bumped to another flight, instead of setting compensation limits, employees are encouraged to make their best judgment based on the situation and the best human response.

Alaska Airlines Lets Employees Make You Whole. #MakeMomProud.

IMPACT: With these tool kits, Alaska Airlines prepares and enables people to act, elevating both the customer and employee experience. People in companies united by purpose, which they prove by action and trust, are the happiest and build the greatest organic growth and results. Smarter Travel, The Points Guy (TPG), and Flyer Talk cite Alaska Airlines as the best of the best in the United States as an airline and/or frequent flyer program. It just earned J.D. Power's highest satisfaction rating among traditional (nonbudget) airlines for the tenth year in a row.

THE MOM LENS

Making Everyone "Customer Rescue Artists" #MakesMomProud.

Alaska Airlines' "empowerment toolkit" gives everyone in the company the ability to be a "customer rescue artist" on the spot—no permission required.

Do You Walk Customers Out of Trouble Spots?

Can Everyone Across Your Company Deliver "We've Got You" Moments?

Dare to Rethink
What's Always Been Done.

Design to improve customers' lives.

"IF I CHIP IN SOME MONEY, WILL YOU GET NEW MAGAZINES?"

Every summer, kids who had advanced during the school year slide a little backward during the summer months. The more than twenty-five million low-income public school students are especially susceptible to this loss of knowledge. During the summer months, they lose, on average, two to three months in reading and math skills, while kids in higher income homes with continued access to reading materials and resources stay steady or make slight gains.

To help these susceptible kids and families in their community, Umpqua Bank initiated an effort called "Stop the Slide." They commit time, funding, and their own resources to provide these kids with tools and education so they keep advancing with their peers.

Unusual for a bank, you might say. But not for a make-mom-proud company. Like Umpqua Bank, these companies hold themselves accountable for helping customers achieve their goals. They are not afraid to rethink what's already been done or walk away from norms that have defined their industries. Umpqua Bank supports its entire community, including customers and those who are not. It takes actions grounded in the belief that, when you contribute to what people care about in their lives, you earn the most honorable type of growth. **Make-mom-proud companies choose to do more.**

In determining their actions, behavior, and their operation, they take a human-centered approach to engaging with customers. Products and services are designed based on their careful understanding of what customers desire and seek to achieve. They understand customer needs, creating a personal and human connection to them. They imagine customers living their lives and design experiences to improve them. Imagining customers in their lives gives them the conviction to rethink what they do and walk away from standard business practices, earning growth through differentiation.

Expanding business by understanding lives.

Careem, the ride-sharing service in the Middle East, for example, thought beyond the borders of other car-riding services in order to find out what was important to meet the needs of their passengers. Upon learning that riders who become parents are uneasy about ride sharing and child and infant safety, they took responsibility to deliver peace of mind to them.

To support this growing population of customers, Careem Kids was born. On their app, customers select Careem Kids as the car type. A car from their dedicated fleet preinstalled with a child seat is then assigned to pick them up. "When our customers book a service with us, our primary objective is to simplify their lives, and when it comes to parents booking a car for their children, we want them to enjoy complete peace of mind," Aura Lunde, general manager of Careem UAE said when describing the service. Careem achieves their goals by helping customers achieve theirs. Through this new experience inspired by the needs of parent riders, customer demand has doubled the "Careem Kids" service.

This is our opportunity to move our priorities out and move customers' goals in. For example, do you know, I mean *truly* know, across your customer journey, what your customers' goals are in each stage? Are you aware of their lives' realities in each? And their desires, needs, concerns? **Are you willing to reinvent your operation to meet customer goals?**

When you dare to rethink what's always been done, challenging and evaluating your operation through the lens of meeting customer goals, inspired products and services will emerge. They will prove to customers that you have their best interests in mind. And these will differentiate you.

This next story highlights the importance of starting with customers' needs, goals, and expectations to design services. For many hotels, a laundry service might suffice. But when your clientele curates its wardrobe like an art collection, and trusts you to care for one-of-a-kind pieces, you need to totally rethink "the laundry."

A Case Study to #MakeMomProud

The Dorchester Hotel Collection Decided to Rethink the Laundry.

DECISION INTENT: Let customer desires lead service design. The Dorchester Collection includes iconic properties such as the Beverly Hills Hotel on Sunset Boulevard, Hotel Bel-Air in Los Angeles, and Hôtel Plaza Athénée in Paris. Their luxury services are developed with a blend of both precision and intuitiveness to cater to customer preferences and desires.

For example, delving into a pattern of social media reviews and consultations with kitchen staff in their restaurants uncovered that 80 to 90 percent of breakfast customers customize their order to cater to their dietary restrictions or lifestyle. Now at the Beverly Hills Hotel, there is no breakfast menu. The waiter asks what you'd like that morning, and whatever your palate desires, it will be yours. Just reading complaints might have driven action to change menu items, rather than the breakthrough action of no menu at all. Ana Brant, who is the global director of guest experience and innovation at the Dorchester Collection, calls this the "relentless pursuit of disruptive insights."

ACTION TO #MAKEMOMPROUD: Establish a wardrobe experience—*not* a laundry service. In her article in the *Harvard Business Review*, Brant describes a similar path that led to the complete reinvention of their laundry service. Digging in after complaints about "laundry services" and a spike in replacement costs for items sent to the service, the question to be answered was not "how to make laundry service better," but "what do guests really need and desire?" Again, starting with just the complaint might have led to incrementally changing a process, but starting with the lives of their guests completely reoriented and elevated the purpose and experience.

Redesigning this experience began by understanding the importance of wardrobe quality and status of clothing items by guests. This knowledge moved the Dorchester Collection hotels to elevate what was previously seen as a "chore" and a relatively low-level task into a prestigious service experience.

The Dorchester Collection Is Inspired by Guests' Lives. #MakeMomProud.

IMPACT: The Dorchester now delivers a *wardrobe experience*, not a laundry service, elevating the outcome for both guest and staff. They invest in expert craftspeople to develop and run the service, and staff members are given education, training, and context for guests' lives by visiting high-end stores where they might purchase their clothing. Packaging and delivery of the garments was elevated, and a personalized note and signature from staff to guest describes the care taken for the garment. With these and other guest-inspired actions and gestures, the Dorchester Collection's guest experience index has increased by 22 percent worldwide.

THE MOM LENS

Willingness to Change to Meet Customer Needs #MakesMomProud.

The Dorchester Collection realized that by understanding their guests' attachment to their wardrobes, they needed to reinvent and elevate their laundry service and experience.

Do You Dare to Rethink What's Always Been Done?

Is It Easy or Hard to Redesign What You Do and How You Do It?

Give Me Choices That Jibe with My Life.

One size does not fit all customers.

Here's what we want in our customer experiences: we want it when we want it, how we want it, and where we want it. Any questions? Sometimes we want retail, sometimes internet. Sometimes we will toggle both. At the same time. Oh, and we want you to know where we've been, and have that information at your fingertips.

Oh, right—we also want service any way we want it.

Easy answer. Hard solution.

As customers, we feel like this is our time to get what we want, right? But the fact of the matter is, a lot of data, culture, and processes have to be worked through to get to this state for any company. So, as your mom would say, pace yourself. Break the work into bite-size pieces. Test and learn. Iterate.

But know, customers will be grateful the closer you can get to offering choices that are right for them—that jibe with how they want to do business with you. When you boil it all down, "give me choices that jibe with my life" has at its core: respect for customers' differing needs and priorities. Here are some companies making progress in building their respect delivery machine.

Respect Delivery Machine

Respecting your desire for service options: Canada Post is reimagining how the post office should function to accommodate people's need for efficiency and speed. They have put in drive-through lanes in some stores to allow fast pickup of packages. Customers drive through, have their bar code scanned, and then pick up their package from a window.

Respecting your need for relevant communication: The Royal Bank of Scotland is working to revitalize and earn back customer trust. It is harnessing customer data to tell customers things like when they might be paying twice for the same service, once packaged with their bank account and again when they opted into the service as an add-on. They also automatically message customers when fixed interest deals are coming to an end. Otherwise the customer would automatically roll into a more expensive variable rate.

Respecting your need for making it easy: Lowes Foods has been innovative with its coupon redemption system. Do you ever wonder if companies really want you to redeem their coupons? Lowes Foods worked to increase redemption by embedding its digital coupons directly into their e-circular experiences. This way, customers can clip or redeem coupons while they shop or plan their list online. They can then see redemptions right away as they are adding products into their carts, without toggling to another website or portal. Forty percent more customers now are redeeming because Lowes has made coupon redemption transparent and easy.

Respecting your need for self-service: Georgia Power developed an app for customers called "My Power Usage." It is a personalized tool that lets customers manage their energy costs. From anywhere, they can check and manage daily energy costs. They are also then sent alerts and information to help eliminate billing surprises.

Respecting your need for service *now*: Nike Support is a Twitter powerhouse. Because they never know when or why people will need help, Nike's Twitter account for service is dedicated to just that: all service, all the time. 24/7/365. And because one language does not fit all, they tweet and speak in seven languages: English, Spanish, French, Dutch, Italian, German, and Japanese.

Our case study company, Sephora, succeeds in delivering every element of the "respect delivery machine" through focusing on their customers' varied needs and desires. They are almost omnipresent in the lives of its zealot customers. But somehow it doesn't seem invasive. They give them the information, options, education, and choices they desire. Research validates that shoppers who buy in-store and online have a 30 percent higher lifetime value than those who shop using only one channel. Sephora beautifully achieves a seamless "every channel" experience without customers ever really feeling like they are "shopping"—but instead, are on some kind of beauty carnival ride they can't stop riding.

A Case Study to #MakeMomProud

Sephora Decided on Generosity, Fun, and Personalization as the Way to Grow.

DECISION INTENT: Be part of customers' lives in a fun, natural way. To its customers, an audience that has mountains of beauty advice via YouTube, Pinterest, and others available to it, Sephora's generosity is what makes it a standout. It wants to show up as playful, helpful, fun, and always available. Its intention for growth is to generously jibe with the lives of its customers.

ACTION TO #MAKEMOMPROUD: Encourage play, trying on, and autonomy. Sephora orchestrates a playful conversation with customers, allowing them to opt in or opt out based on their choice. Most important, it knows that customers want to try before they buy. And for the customers who consider this job one in "putting together" their faces, they can't help but want to play around with the tools Sephora offers. For example, the Sephora Virtual Artist mobile app lets customers scan their faces to give them a Color IQ, a number for easy access to the right products for their skin tone. Or customers can access "expert looks," a bevy of professionally done faces to emulate. And they can save those they want in the "my looks" section of the app, easily shareable with friends, and something key to its community-centric customer base. Sephora Flash finishes the sale in a jiffy (think Amazon Prime for beauty).

Sephora's in-store experience extends the fun and generosity. Relevant messaging connects customers to the goings-on at the store they frequent. In-store appointments with free stylists are confirmed via Facebook Messenger chatbots. Once in the store, the fun continues when customers can take both before and after pictures in a mobile app their stylist updates in real time with info on how they made the magic happen. And the fun no-pressure conversations continue after each visit when customers receive personalized emails with pics, tips, and products to buy.

Sephora Grows Through Generosity and Fun. #MakeMomProud.

IMPACT: Who can resist all of this generosity and play? Not many of Sephora's customers, based on the growth of this retailer. Sephora enjoys 2.25 million Twitter followers, and 491,284 Pinterest followers as of this writing. Its Beauty Talk chat room has 40,000 to 70,000 people logged in at any one time. Store openings are like Mardi Gras for beauty, its most recent bringing in more than 1,000 women who stood in line for hours for the store to open. According to Sephora's most recent quarterly report, it is continuing "a record revenue growth," with about 1,750 retail stores in thirty countries, and opening 70 more in the United States in 2017. Through continual innovations, it now has more than ten million customers.

THE MOM LENS

Giving Customers Choices That Are Right for Them #MakesMomProud.

Because Sephora knows and respects customers' varying needs, it offers options for service, sales, experiences, and communication that deliver to more than ten million zealous customers.

> ## Do You Give Customers Choices That Jibe with Their Lives?
>
> *Does Your Experience Show Up as a Respect Delivery Machine?*

Summarizing
"Put Others Before Yourself."

"A mother is a person who, seeing there are only four pieces of pie for five people, promptly announces she never did care for pie."
—TENNEVA JORDAN

That quote by Tenneva Jordan is at the heart of how the make-mom-proud companies earn their spot in the marketplace and their customers' admiration. They step aside and make their customers' priorities their own. They operate at an elevated level, guided by the belief that achieving their business goals is attached to how much they assist customers in achieving their goals. As a result, they establish a new order of design and decision making that demonstrates to customers and employees:

> * Clarity for how they will support customers' lives.
> * Intuitive and empathetic experience delivery.
> * Innovation guided by customer habits and needs.
> * Fearless redesign of what's always been done.

In this chapter, we explored how companies are bucking the trend and showing up as more human, as more intuitive, and as more of a partner. They are doing this by changing the starting point of their actions—from what the company needs—to what customers and partners desire. We explore clarity of purpose as the necessary glue to steer decisions toward a companywide common goal. The seismic shift that occurs when companies design in grace. How knowing customer life moments and inflection points are key to earning advocates. The requirement to move past one customer size fits all. And the necessity of human-centered design as a competency to become the kind of company that earns customer-driven growth.

The questions to ask are, Does this resemble the path your company is on? Are you earning the right to growth by improving customers' lives? Across your company, are you committing to the fearless redesign of what's always been done, inspired by the fact that to achieve your goals you need to help others achieve theirs?

TAKE ACTION!

Are you achieving your goals
by helping customers achieve theirs?

Chapter 6, "Stop the Shenanigans!," will help you evaluate where you are today. It will serve as a mirror test for you to work through with your company and teams. There you will find each of the opportunities and studies outlined with questions to plot your current state. Your evaluation will help you to plan your actions to nudge your company along to where you want it to be.

Please also go to customerbliss.com, where you can download training videos for these stories, the comics, and a leader guide so you can use this material inside your company.

5.

Take the High Road.

"The best way to learn if you can trust somebody is to trust them."
–ERNEST HEMINGWAY

The make-mom-proud companies are choosing to reverse the trend on business practices that have defined their industries. Through leadership guidance and company actions, they are establishing more *balanced* relationships, where both sides win. Both customer and company are better off because they are in each other's lives.

Three behaviors are common among the make-mom-proud companies as they move in this direction. First, leaders are clear about how they will and will not earn revenue. Leaders diligently take actions to point out exactly what the high road is, creating a path for the company to follow. For example, by refusing to open their stores on Black Friday, REI took a stand to inspire employees and the marketplace. For REI, Black Friday is an outdoor and a family day, not a commerce day. Airbnb takes the high road by showing employees how to embrace the coda "Belong anywhere," building its culture of "belonging."

Next, they choose to be transparent in explaining the "why" behind their actions, such as pricing or how and why they build products the way that they do. By sharing information about their products and their pricing, and by openly transferring knowledge to customers, make-mom-proud companies prove they want to do what's best for them.

When doing research for this chapter, I learned a term that describes this approach to fearlessly sharing, that builds bonds with customers: "radical transparency." In this chapter you'll hear about OVO Energy in the UK, which practices this level of transparency with customers by opening up their pricing plans to the public, outlining exactly what the energy costs are to them, so customers feel equity in what they are paying. As a result, they are earning customer raves and growth.

Transparency, increasingly, is becoming more important to customers, and more differentiating for brands. Another highly praised and unexpected example of radical transparency comes from Sweden. To celebrate its 250-year anniversary of abolishing censorship, the Swedish Tourist Association created a public phone number so that anyone around the world could dial in and speak to a Swedish citizen volunteer in the program.

Citizen participants were encouraged to tell their callers exactly what it's like to live and work in Sweden—with no holding back! They wanted the words of their citizens, without censorship, to be the voice of the country. This action has engaged not only their countrymen, but also people worldwide who have applauded and enjoyed their candor. A 2016 study by Label Insight proves the power that radical transparency can have on a business: 56 percent of those surveyed said they would be loyal to a company *for life* if it provided complete transparency.

Finally, the make-mom-proud companies choose to level the playing field, reducing or eliminating practices where, in the past, customers might have felt that the company was holding most of the cards. They are deliberately resisting or changing industry practices so that customers feel a balanced and equitable partnership, and one based on trust. The story of Luscious Garage in this chapter shows how they bring the technician and customer together, turning the experience into one of collaboration, trust, and even joy.

Some of the high-road actions Make-mom-proud companies take to grow may sound irrational. But repeatedly, examples of their bravery in committing to customer relationships have proved otherwise. They build bonds by the humanity their acts display. For example, when Jet Blue decided to give customers who owed taxes in 2017 a little boost by offering them a free flight coupon, customers were delighted that the airline *did not* ask them for proof of taxes owed. Jet Blue took their customers' word for it. In this chapter, we celebrate those brave companies, such as Jet Blue, who take the high road.

The high road is a choice. And while it's not always the easiest choice, it's the one you'll be happiest about in the rearview mirror. It's the stuff that clearly makes that mom of yours proud.

The high road is also the route to success for companies that take it. Empirical data and anecdotes from customers and employees prove that taking the high road grows a business. Business strategist Fred Reichheld was one of the first to connect the dots between Golden Rule behavior and business growth. Further, Danny Meyer's Hospitality Quotient proves how companies with employees and business practices that deliver values based on human experiences significantly beat the S&P 500. But the key to growing in this manner is leadership. Leaders must build a company that believes that doing the right thing is the right way to grow.

As customers, we desire to give our trust to **companies who trust us back.** We seek out companies whose employees are given permission to do the right thing, and where we are honored as assets. We breathe a sigh of relief and gratitude when "Gotcha!" moments are flipped to "We've got your back" moments. We applaud accountability because we know that everyone makes mistakes. And we thank goodness for the companies who level the playing field and give us information to help us prosper.

Honor and respect forms the backbone of make-mom-proud companies. This chapter showcases companies who question the status quo, change how things are done, and rebuild how they conduct themselves in business. As a result, they earn "goodness-driven growth."

Inspire What You Want Delivered.

Align purpose with action.

"DO YOU THINK I CAN MAKE IT THROUGH
THE GOALPOSTS, ER...I MEAN COLUMNS?"

Nostalgic for his mother's thick and natural yogurt, years after emigrating from the mountains of eastern Turkey, Hamdi Ulukaya got a small business loan in 2007 for $700,000 to make his own yogurt. He bought a Kraft yogurt plant that was about to be shut down to produce his brand, which he named Chobani, meaning *shepherd* in Turkish. At the time, in the United States, we hardly knew what Greek yogurt was—it was only 1 percent of the market. Today, Greek yogurt commands 52 percent of the market, with Chobani as the number one selling brand.

Taking care of employees, using natural ingredients, and doing good in the world are the values of the multi-billion-dollar Chobani company. What makes Ulukaya inspirational is how personally he takes his business. During the first five years of his operation, people who expressed dislike for his yogurt, for whatever reason, received a surprising and very human phone call from Ulukaya, who wanted to make it right.

Ulukaya takes the high road in more ways than one. He also extends his personal commitment to his employees. An inclusive and compassionate leader, he's given every employee a 10 percent stake in the company. Always connecting Chobani's work to the importance of family, he gives six weeks of family leave to both new mothers *and* fathers, including foster and adoptive parents. He takes personal responsibility for living the word *shepherd* by supporting refugee workers, employing hundreds of them, and launching the nonprofit Tent Foundation. Ulukaya has signed Warren Buffett's "giving pledge," committing to giving away the majority of his wealth. Most recently he's started the HUG Initiative to train up-and-coming Turkish entrepreneurs.

Ulukaya has the attributes of a "growth by generosity" leader. But he is also a fierce competitor. And he is now prodding other leaders to grow in the same manner, toggling both humanity and commerce. He is also, like every one of the great leaders we have highlighted in this book, reflective and grounded by the experiences of his childhood, and of his mother. In an interview with *Fast Company*, he said, "There is not a day that goes by that I don't travel back to my childhood." **Does how your mom raised you guide how you lead?**

Align action with purpose.

Leaders who align actions with purpose can move mountains, as Ulukaya did, to start an unexpected business and grow it to the top of its industry. There are many leaders articulating their purpose, but far fewer are in the slog every day working to deliberately translate purpose into action. Here are a few that inspire:

Southwest Airlines CEO Gary Kelly proved he is one of these kinds of leaders when he made a commitment that his airline would no longer sell more tickets than it had seats—not even one. Amid worldwide passenger angst, he initiated what the airline calls *Transfarency*, in which the company pledges to keep low fares without any need for nickeling and diming.

In my conversation with the Southwest Airlines president emerita, Colleen Barrett, she explained how Southwest repeatedly resists the slippery slope of charging for bags, change fees, and other items as other airlines do. They work to squash the temptations that create an unbalanced relationship between customers and their employees.

For companies of all sizes: purpose—and *how* a company lives it— matters. Shane Green, who wrote the great book *Culture Hacker*, states that more than 50 percent of employees leave within the first year of their roles because they don't see their company's stated purpose lived out in the workplace. Would you make a promise to your mom and then not keep it?

The 2017 Deloitte Millennials Survey validates Green's finding that purpose matters. This consumer group of millennials in particular seeks companies whose actions and behaviors display values congruent with their own. I would assert that this desire expands well beyond this intriguing group, that most of us would like to see companies behave with this congruence of "heart and habit."

This is our opportunity to deliberately connect the dots between why a company states that it is in business and its actions to live up to that promise.

REI generated an estimated 6.7 billion media impressions as it fearlessly closed its doors to encourage everyone to #OptOutside on Black Friday. Starting with the simple question "How do we want to show up during the holidays?," read on for more inspiration on how purpose-driven leadership has inspired people and growth.

A Case Study to #MakeMomProud

REI Decided to Opt Out of Black Friday.

DECISION INTENT: Don't double-cross our purpose with commerce. REI believes "that a life outdoors is a life well lived." This guides how it operates, whom it recruits, and how it builds customer relationships. A co-op of sixteen million members forms the "outdoor community" to whom it holds itself accountable. And it is its dedication and commitment to this community that guides REI's behavior. In its most recent Stewardship Report, the company stated that 79 percent of its profits were given back to the outdoor community. This elevates REI to a level far exceeding a purveyor of boots, tents, and other outdoor equipment. It embraces members in achieving a life well lived, with dedication, purpose, and life balance. So when it came to deciding between shopping or spending time outdoors on "Black Friday," there was no contest.

ACTION TO #MAKEMOMPROUD: Closed shop on Black Friday, urging family over commerce. It happened first in 2015 on the shopping day Black Friday, when REI CEO Jerry Stritzke closed shop for all of its 143 stores in a campaign noted as #OptOut. Stritzke explained the action as an investment in getting people outside with the people they care for "over spending it in the aisles." A black screen on the website encouraged people to #OptOut instead of shopping. When this practice was continued the following year, Stritzke said that "our values have not changed." Seen by some as risky for a retailer to walk away from such a significant day, its purpose-driven act delivered financially and beyond, elevating REI in the eyes of its customers and employees.

REI Grows by Sticking to Their Purpose. #MakeMomProud.

IMPACT: REI has earned the respect of members, become a magnet for attracting purpose-driven employees, engaged business and the community, and driven growth. In 2015, 1.4 million people responded to REI's encouragement to step away from shopping and #OptOut, and there were more than 6 million in 2016. More than seven hundred companies have banded together in REI's movement, and hundreds of state parks offered incentives to get people moving and outdoors on Black Friday. Financially, REI continues to grow, where its comparable competitors are struggling.

Culturally, these actions create a stronger workforce, and breed a greater, stronger company. The up-and-coming work generation has been very vocal and deliberate about choosing to work for companies whose values are congruent with their own. And this action by REI has become a magnet for these individuals. Following the initiation of #OptOut, REI saw a 100 percent increase in applications for jobs in its fourth quarter, receiving hundreds of thousands of applications to fill twelve thousand positions. REI's employee retention is double its retail competitors. It has had a place on *Fortune*'s 100 Best Companies to Work For list for nineteen consecutive years.

THE MOM LENS

Proving Your Purpose with Action #MakesMomProud.

REI's purpose to get folks outdoors moves them to take risks to grow differently than business as usual, such as closing their doors on Black Friday because it's an outdoor day and a family day.

> ## Do Leader Behaviors Inspire What You Want Delivered?
>
> *Does Why You're in Business Line Up with How You Act?*

Honor Customers as Assets.

Remember customers, take care of them,
and don't take them for granted.

"IF YOU'RE A NEW CUSTOMER, PRESS '1' FOR
AMAZING LOW RATES, HUGS, AND KISSES. IF YOU'RE A
BORING CURRENT CUSTOMER, HOLD FOR HIGHER RATES."

When a new pet store moved into Jeanine's neighborhood, she was
ecstatic. Her schnauzer, Buddy, was now just minutes from care if he
needed it, and she loved the convenience. The day the store opened,
Jeanine went over to register Buddy, sign up for the loyalty program,
and make an appointment for his first grooming. She continued those
appointments every six weeks like clockwork.

Over the years, Jeanine bought all of Buddy's toys and food from
the store, as well as vitamins, and grooming and pet care services. A
devoted pet mom to Buddy, she was a frequent visitor.

But Jeanine always felt like something was missing in her trips to the store. She felt that Buddy was just a number, not recognized as a "regular." The staff often didn't check records before Buddy's appointment to get to know him or Jeanine.

When Jeanine showed up about seven minutes late for an appointment, Buddy's 105th with the store, she was told that they had moved on to the next dog and she'd have to reschedule. She'd had enough. The staff had her contact information, but made no effort to reach her to find out if she was on her way. They didn't know her, and certainly hadn't tallied up all that she had spent there, or her loyalty to the store. Jeanine stopped shopping there after five years of weekly purchases and constant grooming and care.

Would you take your mom's money for years, and then not recognize her, or cut her a break? Jeanine, like most customers, yearns to know that a company values her consistent business over the years. They want people to honor the relationship. And they certainly want to be recognized and appreciated.

Think of your own life. What's the first thing you think of when a company you've been loyal to treats you like a number? It's "Don't they know how much I spend here," right? If you walked into your favorite restaurant every week and no one recognized you after the fifth trip, how would you feel? Would you eventually stop going?

Remember customers, take care of them, and don't take them for granted.

This is our opportunity to honor customers for how they honor us. Customers can tell when a company is taking them for granted. They offer better rates to new customers, won't honor simple requests or go the extra-mile in appreciation of the relationship, and require customers to repeat who they are over and over again. All of this makes loyal customers wonder, do they value me? Would they even notice if I were gone?

This is our opportunity to say to customers, "We know you; we value you; we realize that without you, we don't have a business." But this requires doing the hard work to know each customer's value. According to Econsultancy, only 42 percent of companies are able to measure customer lifetime value. Those that do measure it behave differently: in enabling their front line to take actions, with how they serve, and in efforts that display gratitude to customers. Make-mom-proud companies give their people the tools to know customer lifetime value, and prepare them with options to ensure that customers *know* that they are valued.

In short, to earn customer loyalty, you must be loyal in return. Alaska Airlines, for example, still awards miles based on miles flown versus ticket price, which is the direction of many airlines. Their commitment to honoring the amount someone is on their planes says to loyal customers, "We value that you fly a lot with us." Not "We value you because you paid more for a ticket."

Here is a story about Bonobos, which has made an art and a science out of understanding, honoring, and growing customer lifetime value. This case study outlines their deliberate path to predict future high-value customers, and the operating model and servicing approach they have taken to honor them and earn customer-driven growth.

A Case Study to #MakeMomProud

Bonobos Decided to Know and Honor Customer Lifetime Value.

DECISION INTENT: Help guys buy pants that fit. Then honor their loyalty. Bonobos started with a pair of chino pants. Stanford MBA student Brian Spaly created a class project where he asked guys, "Do you like your pants?" The resounding answer he got was "No!" From those responses, Brian created the first pair of Bonobos pants. They had a curved waistband to accommodate different builds of men, creating their signature approach to sizing and fit. In 2007, co-founder Andy Dunn joined Spaly to figure out how to sell those pants to men looking for pants that feel just right for them.

Bonobos had a yearning from the beginning to be much more than a company that sells pants. They wanted to take care of their customers and build a relationship with them. Bonobos's founders had a goal to blend the art of fit and "guy conversation" and service, with the science of customer lifetime value to honor their most valued customers. That is why Bonobos has created both online and offline connections. And have become students of understanding which combinations of each create zealous customers.

ACTION TO #MAKEMOMPROUD: Know and honor customers as assets. From its start, Bonobos has been on a quest to *earn* high customer lifetime value, and to know and honor those customers who become their greatest assets. Like many companies, especially retailers where integrated data is scarce, initial calculations were done old school on Excel spreadsheets.

Bonobos's ability to honor customers as assets has matured into a scientific approach, using predictive analytics that unites data across customer touch points to calculate overall customer lifetime value, and lifetime value across twenty-five customer segments. When identified, high-value customers receive personalized services by "Service Ninjas" or with folks at their Guide shop stores, who have their lifetime value information. With this science, Bonobos can predict future high-value customers as early as the first purchase, triggering outreach and service that continues to honor and grow their customer asset. This blend of science and service customizes relationships, builds bonds, and grows the Bonobos business.

Bonobos Knows and Honors Customers as Assets. #MakeMomProud.

IMPACT: By blending the art of service with the science of knowing their customers, Bonobos has increased the predicted lifetime value of its new customers by 20 percent. Never losing sight that service and experience make the formula that earns that growth, they use these insights to expand their place in their customers' lives. Bonobos has become the largest clothing brand ever built on the web. Bonobos was purchased by Walmart in 2017 for $310 million. Andy Dunn, who will continue at the helm, says not to worry. He won't let his fans down and promises to keep the brand's soul.

THE MOM LENS

Honoring Customers as Assets #MakesMomProud.

Bonobos customers are never taken for granted and never forgotten. Bonobos combines science, service, and experience to honor and earn customer lifetime values that continue to grow.

Do Your Actions Honor Customers as Assets?

Does Your Experience Ever Signal That They Are Less Important to You?

Let Two-way Trust Define Your Actions.

Earn customer trust by trusting them back.

"IF I'M TRUSTING THEM WITH MY MONEY, WHY CAN'T THEY TRUST ME WITH THEIR 25-CENT PEN?"

For the Chicago Cubs organization, trust and hope, for many, *many* years, were all the currency they had to give their fans. When they finally won that National League championship title in 2016, it had been 108 years since a Cubs jersey was in a World Series. Since 1906 they had qualified for the post season on only eighteen occasions. Bound together by heartbreak and joy, through generations of families, the Cubs' relationship with their fans is one of reciprocal trust. Both gave and got.

Loving the underdog Cubs was our family tradition, nurtured by my dad. We made many memories within the "friendly confines" of Wrigley Field. When that championship title finally came in 2016, my family—as well as millions of other Cubs fans around the world— were rewarded for trusting that its team would eventually win the championship title. What's more, Cubs fans rewarded their team in return. Millions came out to cheer them on and celebrate. Officials estimate that five million people showed up at the parade and rally held for the Cubs in Chicago, making it, by some estimates, the seventh largest gathering in human history.

The foundational trust that the Cubs built with their fans is not unlike the trust that grows over time between a company and its customers. And while companies may not have millions of people lining the streets to cheer for them, what they end up earning is essentially the same: a two-way, balanced relationship. Even now, writing this shortly after they fell short of making that World Series goal again, hope springs eternal. In Cubs, we trust.

Earn customer trust by trusting them first.

Every customer relationship begins *because* a customer chooses to trust an organization and its people. Physicians are trusted with the health of families; Realtors are trusted to guide a home purchase or sale; computer manufacturers are trusted to provide reliable equipment to do a job; banks are trusted to ensure financial safety and security.

Would you invite your mom over to help make dinner, then chain the blender to the counter? Of course not. Silly question. We don't need to protect our stuff from our moms. But customers *can* feel a lack of trust from companies at times by how offers are structured, their legal wording, or the amount of fine print or conditions for making a sale.

One-sided trust can inadvertently show up in how new customers are evaluated, contracts are negotiated, or in requiring compliance to processes that seem to benefit the company over the customer. This behavior can make the customer feel small and at times defenseless.

You know it in your life as a customer. It's exhausting physically because of the extra time and effort required to make sure you get a fair shake. And it's emotionally exhausting when it feels like companies are trying to protect themselves—from us.

This is our opportunity to earn trust—through giving trust.

Implicit in every customer relationship is a contract of trust. Customers trust that the company will do what it promised, and they seek that trust in return in how the company chooses to do business with them.

Do you work to trust your customers? Do you trust them in your forms, paperwork, and contracts? Are there any clues you give that could indicate a lack of trust, like a pen chained to the desk? Do you have moments where they might think, "They don't seem to trust me"?

Zane's Cycles in Connecticut, for example, embraces two-way trust with potential customers. They trust folks who come into their store for a test ride—by letting them take a bike out for a spin without putting down a credit card first. This gesture says "hey, we know you'll return the bike." At Zane's they don't want to threaten the potential long-term lifetime value of their customers (over $12,500) with a first interaction that questions a customer's integrity. For Zane's this pays off, in both customers who return to buy from those rides, and the lack of bikes they lose—fewer than three per year. And they never lose the expensive bikes that are tested. Trust given is trust returned.

To move closer to a balanced relationship with your customers, consider inventorying your opportunities for giving trust. Identify communication and compliance with processes required across your customer's journey. Identify who holds the power in each and why. Begin to challenge the status quo. Ask the questions your mom would ask. Overturn and redesign for two-way trust.

Now for something completely different, the story of Lemonade Insurance. The guys behind Lemonade Insurance spent a lot of time thinking about *why* insurance just doesn't feel like the greatest experience. Trust is hard in the insurance industry because of all the fine print and the rules and the process around filing a claim. Grounded from its inception on mutual trust, their customer oath of honesty, recorded on video, is all they frequently need to get a claim moving, and sometimes closed, within minutes. Read on for the inspiration!

A Case Study to #MakeMomProud

Lemonade Insurance Decided on an Honesty Pledge.

DECISION INTENT: When you trust people, they trust you back. Lemonade Insurance's mission was to figure out how to square the imbalance of the insurance relationship and the emotional toll that it takes on trust. This begins with how Lemonade gets paid. For the renter and homeowner policies they currently offer, you pay a flat rate calculated by your address, valuables, and so on. To keep their doors open, they take 20 percent off the top. When signing up, customers pick a charity of their choice. This is because of Lemonade's giveback program where—wait for it—the funds remaining after covering their 20 percent and paying claims are divided up to go to each customer's charity of choice. With this element, Lemonade has embedded the sharing and trusting economy into what they do.

ACTION TO #MAKEMOMPROUD: A claim experience fueled by trust. Lemonade's commitment to trust as the fuel for growth guides its approach to claims. For example, let's say your dog ran into a table and broke a beautiful vase that was your grandma's. On the Lemonade app, their 24/7/365 bot AI Jim asks what happened, and why you are putting in the claim. Next he asks you to sign the honesty pledge, vowing to Lemonade, the other members, and the charities who benefit from fairness in reporting that you will do the right thing: "*I understand that I'm part of a community of people who trust each other to be honest. I promise to only claim what I truly deserve. I SWEAR I'LL BE HONEST.*" Finally, this oh-so-smart and "momlike" company asks you to look them in the eye, and record a video giving the reason for your claim. Mom always wanted to hear our side of the story. I have a hunch that's a bit in play here too. From there, sometimes in minutes, your claim is reviewed and paid.

Lemonade Insurance Trusts Their Customers. #MakeMomProud.

IMPACT: "*When you trust people, they trust you back*" guides how Lemonade trusts, and in return, is treated by its customers. For example, a customer put in a claim for a lost laptop and got instant payment. When in a surprise turn of events, the laptop was returned to him, the customer contacted Lemonade to return the previously paid claim. That is a testament to the power of Lemonade's trust-based model. Their acquisition numbers bear this out. On their transparency blog, a recent post shared that Lemonade has captured 27 percent of policyholders who are newcomers to insurance in their currently limited New York market area. Note: This start-up is still young. It will be fun to see how far trust can make a company grow.

THE MOM LENS

Building Relationships Where Both Sides Win #MakesMomProud.

Lemonade made trust their foundation. In their claim process, both company and customers win because their honesty pledge holds both sides accountable for doing the right thing.

Does Two-way Trust Define Your Actions?

Are You Earning Customer Trust by Trusting Customers in Business Practices?

Get Rid of Any "Gotcha!" Moments

Replace them with "We've got your back" moments.

"THIS COUPON IS GOOD ONLY ON TUESDAY,
BETWEEN 4:30 AND 5:00, PAYING WITH CASH,
DURING A LUNAR ECLIPSE."

Suzanne and Bob saw a special in the paper for reduced-price luncheons at their local restaurant. It was sponsored by one of those coupon services, which they had never used before, but thought they would give it a try. Low on disposable income since they had both retired, they looked forward to getting out for a bite, even perhaps making this something they might do every week.

The next Monday they went over to the restaurant for lunch at noon. When their waiter arrived at their table, they told him they were there for the coupon special lunch deal. "Can you excuse me a minute?" the server asked. He returned and broke the bad news: their lunch meal deal was only valid for Tuesdays and Wednesday after 2 p.m. Because this was a Monday at noon, the restaurant, unfortunately, would not honor the coupon.

Suzanne and Bob decided to stay because they were already seated, but the disappointment of their coupon experience lingered throughout the meal. "Why didn't they make that detail clear?" "Why couldn't they just have honored it for us?" Suzanne asked Bob. He didn't know. What he did know was that they wouldn't be going back there or seeking out any more "good deal" coupons.

Create "We've got your back" moments.

What feel like "Gotcha!" moments are often surprise facts that haven't clearly been disclosed to us as customers. As my mother used to call them, these are the "ifs," "ands," or "buts" of the situation. If this . . . , then that . . . , and therefore what you want won't happen. Or if you do this but not that, then what you want won't happen. You get the picture. The Make-mom-proud companies choose to turn these "Gotcha!" moments into "We've got your back moments."

Bob and Suzanne's story did, eventually, have a happy ending. After they had expressed their dismay at the unclear rule preventing them from getting the lunch special, their waiter pled their case to the manager. At the end of the meal, the waiter told the couple that their lunch was on the house. The restaurant had made it too difficult to know how to redeem the deal. The restaurant also decided that they'd continue to honor the coupon for others like Suzanne and Bob who weren't aware of the coupon limits. It made no sense to lose customers over a few dollars on a meal. Especially when the goodwill of honoring the coupon was not only the right thing to do, but the right thing for the business.

Do you have any "if," "and," or "but" conditions that would frustrate your mom? Anything in the products you deliver, the services you provide, the fees you charge, or the specials customers receive? Anything complex or unknown that customers need to decipher? If you do, then you might be delivering a few "Gotcha!" moments to your customers.

This next story is about library overdue fees and one brave library system that bucked the system by getting rid of the overdue fees. Overdue fees actually get in the way of a library's mission, when you think about it. Instead of encouraging people to finish that book, they have to return it to avoid those fees. This was, in fact, a dilemma my mom faced every year when we went on our two-week camping vacation: either let me take out the twenty books needed to sustain me during the trip (book nerd), resigning herself to the late fees, or make me go camping bookless. As I chatted with Alison Circle, the chief customer experience officer at the Columbus Metropolitan Library, I learned that this type of situation is *exactly* why they got rid of those "Gotcha!" overdue fees that get in the way of their mission, which is: "to build a foundation for a successful life." Please enjoy.

A Case Study to #MakeMomProud

Columbus Metropolitan Library Decided They Would Ditch Overdue Fees.

DECISION INTENT: Let young minds grow. "We've had fines for over 100 years, and they are not working," Chief Customer Experience Officer Alison Circle told me. Customers of the library focus on paying those overdue fees, and remember it. And fee rules, such as prohibiting people from taking out a book if they owe more than ten dollars in late fees, turn library staff into cashiers rather than guides to young people. This library said, "Enough with the fees!" The library wanted their patrons to concentrate on getting that great book read or having kids meet their summer reading goals, not shorting time with their books because it was due back with that fee looming.

ACTION TO #MAKEMOMPROUD: They got rid of late fees! No more ten cents a day tracking! The first major urban library in the United States to remove late fees, this action focuses the organization back to its mission. And it removes the "Gotcha!" memory of book fines. Now what people know at their library is that kids can always take out five books at a time, on which they will never incur a fine. And because taxpayers buy the books customers are reading, all the library *really* wants to know is that the book will get back to the library for others to enjoy. Customers have 28 days to return the book, with automatic renewal kicking in, if necessary, giving readers 280 days of grace to read that book. And importantly, this library smartly doesn't count on those

fees as revenue, so eliminating them didn't harm library funding or programs.

Columbus Metropolitan Library Got Rid of "Gotcha!" Late Fees. #MakeMomProud.

IMPACT: *"Removing barriers to get more materials into the hands of more customers brings us closer to achieving our vision of a thriving community where wisdom prevails,"* said the library's CEO Patrick Losinski as he introduced this new approach for the library. Their decision has inspired libraries all over the United States to rethink their overdue-fine "Gotcha!" fees and drop them. And the impact? Circle told me, "The immediate impact has been twofold: customers are relieved of the negative feelings they have had about owing fines; now customer interactions are focused on helping and guiding. Both staff and customers feel a more positive connection. As expected, the change has had minimal impact on finances and other metrics are holding steady. This move has motivated other library systems to follow suit: three neighboring library systems took this step in 2017 with other libraries across the U.S. planning to do the same in 2018."

THE MOM LENS

Getting Rid of Customer "Gotcha!" Moments #MakesMomProud.

Columbus Metropolitan Library eliminated overdue fines because it wanted to stay true to its mission to help young minds grow and let people learn.

Do You Have Any "Gotcha!" Moments That Limit Customer Delight?

What Practices Can You Remove to Stand Out for Customers?

Remove Any "Gullibility Tax."

Share the facts so customers can decide.

"YOUR STRUTS ARE SHOT, YOUR STEERING IS BENT, YOU NEED AN ALIGNMENT, YOUR BRAKES NEED AN OVERHAUL AND YOUR TIRES ARE SHOT. GOOD THING YOU CAME IN FOR THAT OIL CHANGE."

Here's something we may all have experienced in our lives as customers: We contact a company for one thing, and end up being sold much more than we bargained for. Especially when it comes to our highest and most complicated life expenditures, like taking care of our health, our vehicles, or keeping our families secure, we err on the side of accepting more. We accept more because we're worried about what will happen if we don't.

In these situations, we need a navigator, don't we?

We need peace of mind that our lack of understanding is not an opportunity for companies to sell more by appealing to our concern and desire to do the right thing for our families and ourselves. We just don't want to pay a "gullibility tax" where we overpay because of un-certainty and fear.

Share the facts so customers can decide.

Make-mom-proud companies guide customers through the com-plexity of pricing, and sell them only what they need. They earn the right to growth by navigating customers fearlessly toward the solu-tions best for the customer. They deliver education, complete infor-mation, and plain and simple facts so customers can decide what they really *do* need. These companies give customers the full story. They give them options. They make customers smart, so they can decide.

Overselling may work when our customers are vulnerable. But it won't earn peace of mind or word-of-mouth or continued customer growth when they reflect on their experience, tell friends, and share it on social media.

This is our opportunity to grow through transparency and trust. **Do you have any "gullibility tax" moments in your business?** Luscious Garage in San Francisco is a company that has figured out how to improve a customer experience in which most of us have experienced a "gullibility tax" in our lives: taking our car in for ser-vice. They built a business that turned the experience of getting a car repaired from one of fear and worry to one of honor and trust. Caro-lyn Coquillette, the owner of Luscious Garage, says that the car ser-vice experience is 70 percent about the customer and 30 percent about the car. And she has *such* a point there. Think about it: it's the emotional fear of going to get service, the back and forth or nonexis-tent communication, and the never-sure-about-it pricing that always seems to mark that car repair experience. Luscious got rid of all that—on purpose.

A Case Study to #MakeMomProud

Luscious Garage Decided Job #1 Was "Repairing" Customer Trust.

DECISION INTENT: Lose the old school car service experience. Luscious Garage owner Coquillette says that "part of fixing the customer is getting them over their prior repair horror stories." So Luscious decided from its inception that they would forge relationships that begin with understanding the past service experiences of the customer standing before them. From there, the job is to fix that customer's trust in a service experience with actions—proving that they will only do what is necessary, that the fee will be fair, and that their car will be fixed. Getting that done is what builds their hordes of loyal customers. They Make-mom-proud by telling the truth, communicating straight, and honoring people's intelligence.

ACTION TO #MAKEMOMPROUD: "No hiding anything" collaboration. At Luscious, there's no game of "telephone" between the customer adviser, the technician, and the customer. The customer meets directly with the technician responsible for the repair. They look each other in the eye, communicate, and connect as people. They create their game plan together. What happens next as that game plan is executed builds peace of mind and that elusive trust. It is an "our records are your records" experience.

Luscious has built an online and mobile platform for communication that brings the customer into the repair experience with the technician. This makes the customer a collaborator with the technician throughout the process as her vehicle is being diagnosed.

The customer is part of the conversation in real time as the technician guides the customer to go into the same system she is working on to see the findings, the recommendations, and pictures or videos of the problem. Then, in real time, customer and technician collaborate online, reach decisions, and work the plan. This creates a totally different kind of conversation, removing the imbalance between the customer and service repair shop. Much different from that call explaining all the things wrong with your car, the big bill you weren't expecting, and the not knowing what just hit you.

Luscious Garage Wants You to Know What They Know. #MakeMomProud.

IMPACT: They make car repair a collaborative relationship between the technician and the customer. Luscious Garage has an average score of five-stars on Yelp (let that sink in), a smattering of which are included here. Notice the good behavior called out in each: "I felt very confident I was being taken care of by a truthful expert." "Here, you are treated as an equal, like a person." "No oversell. . . . If something isn't needed, they tell me it can wait. . . . Trust and expertise keep me coming back!" "The finest operation, of any kind, with which I've ever done business." Through doing business in this manner, and the love of its zealous customers, Luscious Garage has grown to an estimated $1.5-million-a-year operation for its single location.

THE MOM LENS

Guiding Customers, and No Overselling, #MakesMomProud

Luscious Garage transformed the car repair experience from one of fear and worry to one of honor and trust, with open communication and their technician-customer partnership.

Have Any "Gullibility Tax" Situations in Your Business?

Are Customers Always Navigated to the Right Solution for Them?

Reduce the Nickeling and Diming
or "Opportunity" Pricing.

Charge what is fair, not what is possible.
People will love you for that.

ONLY 30 TIMES MORE EXPENSIVE THAN GASOLINE, WHICH NEEDS TO
BE LOCATED, DRILLED, REFINED, AND DELIVERED IN TANKER TRUCKS.

On a recent afternoon visit to the movies, Joe skipped his usual practice of printing his ticket at home, opting to buy it at the theater.
Much to his surprise, he was informed at the ticket booth that customers who buy at the booth versus printing at home were charged a
new three-dollar service fee. Captive in that moment, Joe paid the
three bucks. But he remembered how he felt, not about the three dollars really, but about the opportunity the theater had taken to get a
little bit more money out of his pocket. Joe told everyone he knew.
And even though he could "work around" the fee and print out the

tickets at home for future visits, he found himself avoiding that the-ater. It just didn't sit right with him.

Charge what is fair, not what is possible.
People will love you for that.

Joe experienced what many of us face at times in our lives as cus-tomers: "opportunity" pricing. The theater used his immediate need for a ticket as an opportunity to charge him more for getting his ticket at the booth. As in Joe's experience, "opportunity" pricing impacts customers not only in their pocketbook but also in their impression of a company. To customers, "opportunity" pricing feels like "They know I have no choice." "I have no choice but to buy this blanket on the plane because I'm cold; no choice but to buy this expensive bottle of water because I'm thirsty; no choice but to pay this exorbitant gas price because I'm out of time before my rental is due—and there are no other options."

Make-mom-proud companies think long and hard before adding on extra fees or bumping up pricing because they can. They ask them-selves: Is it worth overcharging a customer for a bottle of water or a blanket or add on a fee in the long run? Is earning an extra six dollars on a bottle of water worth possibly losing a valuable customer in the future? Is it worth their Instagram pictures and tweets that they share?

"Opportunity" pricing is a slippery slope. I know it's easy to get ad-dicted to the potential upshot of increasing pricing or fees for custom-ers when looked at from the internal company financial perspective. Companies get addicted to the projected revenue increase achievable with fees and charging customers more than necessary in captive mo-ments of need. But that revenue has a cost to be factored in: custom-ers who think less of you . . . and over time, start seeking alternative solutions to your products and services.

I recently had a laugh in my hotel room over "opportunity" pricing. The hotel had included a coffeemaker with my room (nice), but had shrink-wrapped the coffee pod *inside* the cup with a big seven-dollar sticker on top. No coffee for me unless I paid seven bucks for that pod. Not nice. Thousands and thousands of people have now seen the picture of that cup on social media, and it's a hotel I'll try to avoid in the future. Isn't there a better way to grow? **Would you charge your mom what's *fair* for that coffee, or what's *possible*?** Do you have any opportunistic pricing that has seeped into your business?

And now a story that had me giggling with joy (yes, I'm that weird) when I found it. Virgin Hotels has banned the crazy minibar pricing. Instead, they offer guests Mom-approved "street pricing": You get charged only what it would cost you to run down to the local minimart or grocery store to buy that candy bar you've just got to have. Instead of making you wonder about their motives for making money, they build fans that are raving all over the internet about this practice that bucks the trend.

A Case Study to #MakeMomProud

Virgin Hotels Decided on "No Nickeling and Diming" at the Minibar.

DECISION INTENT: Don't take advantage—be fair. You're in your hotel room and wake up in the middle of the night with a terrible thirst. It's dark and you don't check the price of that bottle of water, but as soon as you twist off the cap, you know what you're in for. I always pause at this moment, to decide if I'm going to give in to that price. And I wonder, "Why do they do that?" Don't you?

From the beginning of imagining the Virgin Hotel experience, Richard Branson and CEO Raul Leal were clear that their experience would break away from some standard habits in the hotel industry. They would remove those that cause pain and prompt guests to question the company's intention for how they would earn a profit. In particular, Virgin Hotels would not take advantage of customers by opportunistically imposing charges. They would get rid of the nickeling and diming.

ACTION TO #MAKEMOMPROUD: Minibar "street pricing." In a video on the Virgin Hotel website, Leal says, "You're staying in your room, you can't order room service because it's after midnight and you want a snack. You take some M&M's out of your minibar and it's $6!" This pain point is what Virgin says no to, with an act of fairness that sends a signal about who they are and how they were raised. Their "street pricing" is based on "what you pay at the store, you'll pay at our minibar."

At Virgin Hotels, you'll feel OK opening that can of Coke or bag of chips. They've erased that flinching moment connected with most minibar indulgences: the lack of fairness in the price. "It's not how we were raised to take advantage, and it's not at work here."

Being fair by eliminating nickeling and diming goes beyond the minibar at Virgin Hotels. There is no charge for Wi-Fi. "Bandwidth is a right, not a revenue stream," they say. You also won't get dinged for room service fees, or add-on service charges. And there are no fees for early or late check-in. "We shouldn't feel like 'we've got you,'" Leal says in rebuffing fees experienced at other hotels.

Virgin Hotels Won't Nickel and Dime You. #MakeMomProud.

IMPACT: After only its first year of business, the Virgin Hotel in Chicago was named the number one hotel in the United States by the Condé Nast Traveler Readers' Choice Awards. Condé Nast also named the Virgin Hotel in Chicago to the sixth spot of the top fifty hotels in the world. Do you have any moments where you nickel and dime customers, or take advantage of opportunity pricing—because you can? Can you take the long view as Virgin Hotels does to grow through value versus fees?

THE MOM LENS

Resisting Nickeling and Diming Practices #MakesMomProud.

Virgin Hotels decided that they would not partake in the long-standing hotelier practice of charging customers six bucks for a candy bar because they could. People are cheering. Loudly!

Do You Practice Any Nickeling and Diming on Customers?

Are You Charging What's Fair, or What's Possible Because You Can?

Make Your Apology Your Finest Hour.

How you apologize is your humanity litmus test.

MAKE YOUR APOLOGY YOUR FINEST HOUR.

When challenges hit an organization, how leaders respond tells employees how to respond. It gives the entire company the values they are to uphold when things go wrong. And when smaller things occur, and employees are given the ability to make amends with their dignity intact, it lifts the spirit of everyone.

Mary Barra, who is now CEO and chairman of General Motors (GM), inherited a situation that didn't even happen on her watch. She inherited the very sad situation where more than one hundred customers lost their lives because of ignition switch failures, which eventually led to the recall of 2.6 million Cobalt vehicles. A situation that was ten years in the making, it erupted in the marketplace just days after Barra became CEO.

Barra's response to this situation made a difference for employees inside GM and put a new, human face toward the public and marketplace. Even though she inherited the situation, Barra took accountability for it. She met with the families of the victims to openly discuss the situation and personally apologize. She set up a compensation fund for them prior to any legally required judgment. In all of her public communications, she committed not only to address the vehicle situation failure, but also the cultural and process failures that had led to such a prolonged and delayed reaction.

Barra set a tone in the wake of a tough situation that established how she would hold not just herself but the entire company accountable. Employees saw Barra in call centers taking calls and listening in and speaking with employees, hearing them out, and talking to them about the tragedy. "Something went wrong with our process in this instance, and terrible things happened," she said in her video message to employees. "We will be better because of this tragic situation if we seize the opportunity. And I believe we will do just that." **Barra's courage** gave her entire company the values they are to uphold, when unity and solidarity in her organization mattered the most.

How you apologize is your humanity litmus test.

When companies fall on hard times, we want to see acts of humility and accountability. We want to see empathy and swift, fearless communication, and explanations of the facts that occurred. We want to see leadership behavior we can be proud of: that the company we are a part of is putting customers back together again.

How companies and individuals respond to these situations *does* affect business results. For GM, Mary Barra's changes drove renewed accountability. And most important, they buoyed the spirits of employees observing her very human approach to accountability. She has

put GM on a path to consistently meet or exceed its financial commit-
ments. GM has seen three years of record earnings since she's been
at the helm, and most recently earned a position in *Fortune* magazine's top ten list of America's profitable companies.

Often it's the big public mistakes made by a company that get the
attention. But customers' memories are more frequently formed
through thousands of everyday moments and glitches that might interrupt their experience with a company. In both the large and small
circumstances where we need to mend fences with our customers,
employees need to be given permission to do the right thing—and be
heralded for it.

When issues happen in your company, how do you enable people
to respond? Do you give people permission to act, to take pride in
doing the right thing? Are responses packaged for PR consumption,
or do you communicate from a place of deep responsibility? Do you
take accountability for putting customers' lives back together? **Would
your apologies make Mom proud?**

What I love about this next story is that it demonstrates a continual practice of making things right. The Four Seasons daily "glitch
report" process recognizes that resolving everyday glitches is the constant work that unites and elevates teams and organizations. Little
mistakes don't get the chance to fester. Daily learning drives daily
improvement. And people are given the power to do the right thing to
improve.

A Case Study to #MakeMomProud

The Four Seasons Decided to Always Make It Right.

DECISION INTENT: Constantly achieve the highest standards of service. The Four Seasons is always seeking opportunities to improve their customers' experiences. The day-to-day glitches that customers might experience offer them the chance to constantly level up and increase service, and resolve underlying issues. When addressed swiftly and earnestly, they provide an opportunity to blend empathy and accountability for continual experience improvement. "Glitch moments" that are responded to and resolved, and repair the customer relationship, positively affect customer growth. Isadore Sharp, founder of Four Seasons, puts the emphasis on the outcome of every glitch in the right place. "What's important with the glitch is not the error—it's the recovery," he says.

ACTION TO #MAKEMOMPROUD: The "glitch report."

The Four Seasons has developed a process at each of their locations across the world that routinely eliminates these glitch moments. At the end of every shift, the staff team discusses any glitches that occurred for customers. This process lets people check their worry about what happened at the door, focusing on the recovery to elevate service. Each glitch discussion is centered on what occurred, who apologized to the guest, and what actions were taken to repair the emotional connection and make it right. Shift leaders engage the entire property team in summarizing the glitches so they can be resolved as a team.

Every morning a summary of all the previous day's glitches is discussed.

What strikes me as powerful about this glitch report process is that it is a constant boosting up of service. It serves as a powerful blend of humanity and accountability. People recount the glitches in terms of customer experience and disappointment. Individuals own up to the glitches and take accountability. Then teams band together to make improvements and support each other. Conducted as an improvement effort rather than a punitive one, it encourages and develops the people who have already been hand selected to be a part of the Four Seasons guest experience. This process gives employees, whom Sharp calls "our best product," the gift of enabling the Four Seasons to continue to rise. It gives them the opportunity to create the memory of the recovery, delivering on the Golden Rule foundation that guides behavior there.

The Four Seasons Makes it Right for Customers. #MakeMomProud.

IMPACT: The Four Seasons has one of the lowest turnover rates in the hotel industry. This is because they hire people who possess what Sharp calls "a service heart and aptitude." They've also earned their low turnover rates by creating a work environment that allows people to rise to their best self, he says. The Four Seasons has been ranked in *Fortune* Magazine's 100 Best Companies to Work For list for eighteen years straight. Do you focus on and improve the glitches every day that will encourage your people and company to improve?

THE MOM LENS

Solving Mistakes Every Day #MakesMomProud.

Every day Four Seasons teams identify customer experience glitches. With every shift they identify the issues, solve them, and enable the front line to be the hero for the customer.

Are You Actively Working to Solve Mistakes?

Do You Improve Glitches That Happen with Customers Every Day?

Use Truth and Transparency
to Sell and Serve.

Focus on earning the relationship—not making the sale.

"PAY NO ATTENTION TO THOSE BARS. NOW, ABOUT THE
RUSTPROOFING PACKAGE FOR YOUR NEW CAR..."

Would you make your mom sit in a windowless room for hours, providing information that is confusing, unclear, and a little bit frightening? Would you push her to an extended warranty, then offer fuzzy math on her trade-in and unclear information on how you calculated her monthly payment?

How companies approach some purchases is a reflection of the priorities guiding the organization. And there's a choice to be made here: a company can focus on *making* the sale or on *earning* the relationship.

Make-mom-proud companies work to replace tactics with establishing a relationship. They aim to guide customers. They educate customers with facts, which they've clearly laid out, so they can make informed decisions.

EARN the relationship—don't make the sale.

Think about your life as a customer and the last complicated purchase you made. If you were clearly and openly guided to options and the pros and cons of each, you left with peace of mind not only about what you purchased, but also about the people who guided you through the purchase. But if you were offered packages that you couldn't unbundle or kept scratching your head trying to do the math or make the "deal" make sense, you felt differently. If you've ever had a sales experience that you just wanted to be over, you know what I mean. Think about your sales processes and ask yourself: **Would your mom feel good about how you sold her something?**

What's interesting is that these complicated purchases are important in our lives. We save for them, plan for them, and anticipate them. You can take steps to remove the fear that sometimes creeps up for customers out of the equation.

When you choose tactics, it sets the tone for how employees and the organization respect customers, and condones treatment that defines the kind of company you are. Sales tactics may get you a short-term sale (once), but respect, transparency, and guidance will earn a long-term customer—both their advocacy and growth.

The make-mom-proud companies know that having customers agree to something they were not aware of is not how they will grow long term. And research validates this. The 2016 Label Insight Transparency ROI Study found that almost 94 percent of consumers said that they would be loyal to companies who commit to and behave with complete transparency.

OVO Energy in the UK, from the very beginning, decided that

they wanted to show up like a trusted friend and not a traditional energy company. Born in 2009 on the kitchen table of a few friends in Gloucestershire, England, OVO wants to become the world's most trusted energy brand. And they are doing the work to march toward earning it. They know that to earn trust, you have to trust. To be a friend, you have to act like one.

Here is how they have changed almost everything that people are used to about how they buy, communicate, and pay for energy.

A Case Study to #MakeMomProud

OVO Energy Decided Openness and Honesty Is the Way to Grow.

DECISION INTENT: Show up like a trusted friend. OVO founder Stephen Fitzpatrick and team were very deliberate about how the company would have to behave to become trusted. They had to keep things simple (no hide-and-seek on *anything*). They had to be honest. They had to price fairly. They had to treat customers like they were raised to do . . . decently (his words). Having made those initial promises at the kitchen table of friends, that table now sits in their offices, to make sure that as they grow, their conscience and behaviors keep driving them.

ACTION TO #MAKEMOMPROUD: Four simple energy plans. And NO rigmarole. OVO Energy's goal is to "make the energy industry easier for consumers to understand and make sure prices reflect the actual cost of doing business so they know they're getting a good deal." As a result, what you get immediately from OVO is simplicity in pricing and explanation. And language that sounds like you might even have written it yourself. You choose from simple plans that spell out what you get and what you don't—with no surprises. And OVO doesn't save their best deals for new customers. What you see is what everyone has to choose from. No playing favorites. Oh, and they pay 3 percent interest on any credit balance you hold in your account.

This story is testament to their fairness in pricing to the consumer, based on what they pay. In 2014, the largest energy suppliers in the UK had all increased energy prices,

raising much uproar among consumers. Speaking at an Energy and Climate Change Committee at the time, Fitzpatrick said, "I can't explain any of these price rises." OVO, he went on to say, would <u>not</u> be raising prices at that time, because their cost of wholesale electricity and gas had not risen. They would not raise prices unnecessarily. "Above all, openness and honesty" the team had said they would live by when they started OVO. That kitchen table certainly keeps them grounded.

OVO Energy Gives It to You Straight. #MakeMomProud.

IMPACT: Since entering the market, OVO has grown to nearly seven hundred thousand customers and created more than a thousand jobs. They are the uSwitch Energy supplier of the year for the past three years, and have been named to the *Sunday Times*'s Best Companies to Work For. On Trustpilot, where consumers rate a company's behaviors and relationship, their 8,208 reviews have rated them an average of 8.8/10. In 2016, they posted their first "meaningful profit" according to the company. In 2017, it was reported that they had achieved average growth of more than 220 percent over the past five years.

THE MOM LENS

Transparency in Selling Practices #MakesMomProud.

OVO Energy shows up like a trusted friend in how they sell and serve. Their prices reflect the cost of doing business, which they share, so customers always know that they're getting the right deal.

Does Your Sales Process Help Customers Prosper?

Do You Focus on Earning the Relationship, Not Making the Sale?

Summarizing
"Take the High Road."

As my research on this book deepened, and the make-mom-proud company stories began to take shape, a commonality emerged about how they choose to conduct themselves. And that is they earn "goodness-driven growth." They choose to walk away from or participate in business practices that create an imbalanced customer-company relationship.

The high road is a choice. And while it's not always the easiest choice, it's the one you'll be happiest about in the rearview mirror. These companies take deliberate actions in order to:

* Build balanced relationships.

* Act from honor and respect.

* Practice "radical transparency."

* Earn goodness-driven growth.

In this chapter, we celebrate bravery in reversing business trends. And leadership behaviors exhibited as companies make choices on how they will and will *not* grow. Their leaders inspire people to rise by acting bravely and giving them permission to follow. They give their people the ability to truly honor customers as assets—as the foundation for their growth.

Two-way trust defines the give and take of relationships across customers, employees, partners, and in the marketplace. They are relentless in eliminating legacy practices or "always done it that way" actions to redefine what good behavior in their particular industry should be. In short, they challenge the status quo, rebuilding how they conduct themselves in business to earn goodness-driven growth.

Does your company have a similar path to growth? Are you choosing to build a balanced relationship where both sides win? Are the actions you take earning a marketplace position that reflects who you are and what you value as people?

TAKE ACTION!

Are your company behaviors and actions
earning goodness-driven growth?

Chapter 6, "Stop the Shenanigans!," will help you evaluate where you are today. It will serve as a mirror test for you to work through with your company and teams. There you will find each of the opportunities and studies outlined with questions to plot your current state. Your evaluation will help you to plan your actions to nudge your company along to where you want it to be.

Please also go to customerbliss.com, where you can download training videos for these stories, the comics, and a leader guide so you can use this material inside your company.

6.

Stop the Shenanigans!

#MakeMomProud

"You're off to Great Places!
Today is your day!
Your mountain is waiting,
So . . . get on your way!"
—DR. SEUSS, *OH, THE PLACES YOU'LL GO!*

Hello again, friend.

We're near the end of our time together. But before you go, I wanted to leave you with this assessment to help you reflect on where you are today, so you can take your company, your department, or yourself to where you want to go.

Throughout this book, we've traveled through many of the experiences that define our lives as customers. You've seen examples from large, medium, and small companies and learned how their clarity, bravery, and deliberate actions affect customers, employees, and the marketplace. Following each story has been a "Mom Lens" capturing what that company did to "Make Mom Proud," along with challenge questions to help you to reflect on your work, your company, and how it compares with each of our case study companies.

Now you'll have the chance to choose your own path. Each of the four chapters is recapped here for you, with a summary and a set of questions to ask inside of your company.

All thirty-two case studies are summarized, with a few challenge questions for you to reflect on where you are now, and a **"#MakeMomProud-O-Meter"** you can use to facilitate spirited conversations—discussing the experiences you deliver to customers, employees, and the marketplace.

As always, imagine Mom as you answer the following questions to determine where you are now. And chart your path to goodness-driven growth.

"Be the Person I Raised You to Be."

Empathy and humanity in how you serve.

Our humanity: our humanness, more than ever before, needs to show through in how we do business with customers and each other. But an app alone will not solve everything. With the stratospheric increase in high-tech solutions to "take care" of customers, the need for high touch has also escalated. Customers need a healthy dose of both.

The make-mom-proud companies find the people whose upbringing and values align with what they want their companies to stand for. And then they enable them to bring that version of themselves to work. Selecting who will, and will not, become members of these companies is job number one. But after that, the focus is to help them prosper: to enable them to achieve, and be true to how they were raised.

Make-mom-proud Questions:

Do we enable our people to prosper?

Do we make it easy, and a joy, to deliver care, empathy, and value?

Do We Honor the Dignity of Customers' Lives?

Do we show up as a "caring" company?

The Cleveland Clinic elevates everyone in its organization to "caregiver," giving people the tools, the authority, and the honor to work together so that patients rarely even have to ring that call light. It makes Mom proud by "managing the 360," uniting everyone to care for the total patient experience. And it leads to prosperity, ranking this hospital system as one of the top two in the United States.

· Do we guide cross-company behaviors to build a "caring" organization?
· Are we nurturing our frontline caregivers?
· Have we united everyone to care for customers, regardless of role?

#MakeMomProud-O-Meter

OH DEAR. ☐ ☐ ☐ ☐ ☐ SO PROUD!

Do We Trust the Front Line to Extend Grace?

Can we enable policy and the Golden Rule to collide?

Oberoi Hotels hires people whose values align with their Dharma, their code of ethics. And then they make Mom proud by guiding, trusting, and enabling them to make the right call to honor and grow their customers with appropriate responses. Trusting and holding people accountable to take the right action leads to customer admiration, continued growth of "Promoters," and honor—it's one of India's best places to work.

· Do we prepare employees with customer data and training to make the right call?
· Do we recognize and reward actions that keep valued customers?
· Do we enable people to act with honor and make exceptions when warranted?

#MakeMomProud-O-Meter

OH DEAR. ☐ ☐ ☐ ☐ ☐ SO PROUD!

Do We Hire People with the Ability to Care?

Is hiring our most important decision?

Pal's Sudden Service restaurant screens for the aptitudes and attitudes we learned as kids in their hiring process. They are zealots in ensuring that only those who fit their culture are invited to a place on the team. Taking deliberate steps to build a united culture through hiring makes Mom proud. And for Pal's it leads to employee turnover that is one-third the industry average. Pal's culture is their prosperity engine.

· Do our interviews go beyond questions or skills to know the human behind the résumé?
· Have we established the characteristics of those who belong with us?
· Do we have a process for selecting those who live our values?

#MakeMomProud-O-Meter

OH DEAR. ☐ ☐ ☐ ☐ ☐ SO PROUD!

Are We Doing Any Survey Score Begging?

Do we focus on improving customers' lives, to earn the score?

Safelite AutoGlass focuses on coaching behavior that lifts up both employees and customers. By focusing on people first, the score is earned—but it's never the focus. Focusing on customers' lives and not that survey score makes Mom proud. And admitting that there is improvement to be had makes her even prouder. Building the Safelite spirit helps Safelite become the key player in their industry.

· Do we ever put our people in the position of begging for scores?
· Do we ever send communication to customers asking for a good score?
· Is our customer experience compensation only about survey scores?

#MakeMomProud-O-Meter

OH DEAR. ☐ ☐ ☐ ☐ ☐ SO PROUD!

Do We Check Our Bias at the Door?

Is growth earned through inclusive and respectful behavior?

ThirdLove is a deliberately inclusive brand. They make Mom proud by recognizing every woman's skin color in their product offering. And earn their growth through respectful product design, and honoring all women. This approach contributes to how FirstLove has prospered, experiencing triple-digit growth while competitors experience market decline.

· Are we aware of and do we work to eliminate unconscious bias with customers?
· Do we actively work to remove any bias in our industry?
· Do we prepare our people to remove unconscious bias with each other?

#MakeMomProud-O-Meter

OH DEAR. ☐ ☐ ☐ ☐ ☐ SO PROUD!

Do We Have Any Rules That Inhibit People's Ability to Serve?

Do we nurture frontline heroes, rather than policy cops?

Vail Resorts bans service scripts or penning people into rules that diminish their spirit. They work instead to foster joy. They make Mom proud by getting rid of rules and language that is more about policy than purpose. Vail Resorts earn their place as the premiere ski vacation because they nurture and free employees to deliver the "experience of a lifetime."

· Do we ever say, "Our policy is . . ." to customers?
· Do we give employees the tools to be communicators and problem solvers? To deliver joy?
· Do we work with employees to remove rules that inhibit and diminish their spirit?

#MakeMomProud-O-Meter

OH DEAR. ☐ ☐ ☐ ☐ ☐ SO PROUD!

Do We Reward for Congruence of Heart and Habit?

Do we celebrate people for bringing the best version of themselves to work?

H-E-B Grocery Company is an irreplaceable fixture in the lives of the customers it serves because it recognizes and rewards honorable, gutsy, and noble behavior. H-E-B makes Mom proud because it trusts and praises people who take a chance. It honors congruence of heart and habit in how leaders lead. Prosperity of the human spirit earns its place on *Forbes*'s 100 Best Places to Work list.

· Do we reward and recognize employees for their ability to care?
· Do we celebrate taking risks, doing the right thing, and making informed decisions?
· Do our leaders model, celebrate, and promote people for their human, caring behavior?

#MakeMomProud-O-Meter

OH DEAR. ☐ ☐ ☐ ☐ ☐ SO PROUD!

Do We Nurture Memory Makers?

Can they deliver memories we'd want our mom to have?

Union Square Hospitality Group hires people for their humanity. Technology enhances, never replaces, the beating heart. They make Mom proud because they focus on how you feel when you are seated at their table. Sound like someone you know? USHG prospers by nurturing and keeping memory makers—its turnover rate for full-time employees is about 19 percent annually, compared with an industry average of 27 percent.

· Do we hire people for their intuition, spirit, and ability to deliver a memory?
· Are employees given the time, information, and permission to be memory makers?
· Do we know, prepare our people, and deliver the customer memories that matter most?

#MakeMomProud-O-Meter

OH DEAR. ☐ ☐ ☐ ☐ ☐ SO PROUD!

"Don't Make Me Feed You Soap!"

How easy is it to do business with you?

The Make-mom-proud companies are always on the look-out for "bar of soap" moments they can remove from customers' lives. As customers, they've lived them, and they feel the frustration they create, so they work to eliminate them from the experiences they deliver.

And, of course, all "bar of soap" moments eventually roll onto the feet of your front line. Customers ask: Where is it? How long will it take? Why can't you do that? What does this mean? Why don't you have my records? Why was I charged this fee? Can you waive it? Will you really help me? Can you get me out of this contract?

"Make Mom Proud" Questions:

Do we have any "bar of soap" moments in our experience?

Do we make it easy or hard to do business with us?

Do We Honor Customers' Time, and Their Clock?

Is our business run on "customer time"?

Sweetgreen is on a mission to deliver healthy food fast, but with a dose of humanity. They make Mom proud because they honor people's time and their clock, not their own. Zealot customers who love their food, their approach, and their heart have grown their operation to more than seventy-five restaurants in ten years.

· Do we take customers' time to get basic services accomplished?
· Do we ever make customers wait for us?
· Do we give customers control of their time?
· Do our customers feel like we honor their time and their schedules?

#MakeMomProud-O-Meter

| OH DEAR. | ☐ | ☐ | ☐ | ☐ | ☐ | SO PROUD! |

Do We Take the Monkey Off Our Customers' Back?

Are we reducing service exhaustion?

Virginia Mason's Spine Clinic puts all the pieces together for their patients so that the patients don't have to. They make Mom proud because they have taken the burden off of their customers' backs. They shoulder the work of uniting caregivers, actions, and records. Prosperity has followed, reducing unnecessary procedures and increasing revenue and productivity for both patients and health-care providers.

· Do we make it easy on the customer to solve situations?
· Do we make them do the work?
· Do they have to repeatedly call and research to find the answer?

#MakeMomProud-O-Meter

| OH DEAR. | ☐ | ☐ | ☐ | ☐ | ☐ | SO PROUD! |

Do We Take Disruptions in Customers' Lives Personally?

Do we ever leave customers in the dark?

CenterPoint Energy in Houston delivers proactive communication when the power goes out and things go dark. They make Mom proud because they work to remove the emotional angst of not knowing, and instead inform, communicate, and support. As a result, they prosper—earning trust, high ratings, and raves from grateful customers.

· Are we actively communicating when the unexpected happens and the power goes out, planes are canceled, appointments are rescheduled, or shipments are late?
· Do we reach out first, before customers, when service is disrupted?
· Do we give customers options for how to communicate with and reach us?
· Do we keep customers apprised, and give them peace of mind?

#MakeMomProud-O-Meter

OH DEAR. ☐ ☐ ☐ ☐ ☐ SO PROUD!

Do We Let Customers Depart Gracefully?

Would our departure experience earn an eventual return?

The Casper mattress company knows that a graceful departure can lead to an eventual return. They make Mom proud with their generosity in giving one hundred days to try one of their beds, and a painless and dignified approach to taking it back if it's not right for you. Their unexpected behavior earns prosperity, with growth to more than $500 million in just five years. And kudos to the company as a runner up to *Inc.* magazine's Company of the Year, 2016.

· Do we penalize customers for departing?
· Do we give customers a seamless, simple, transparent way to depart?
· Would customers return to us, based on our treatment?

#MakeMomProud-O-Meter

OH DEAR. ☐ ☐ ☐ ☐ ☐ SO PROUD!

Do We Make It Easy to Get Help?

Is our availability a reflection of how much we care?

Chewy.com knows that pet parents need reliability in service. They make Mom proud by providing always available, always informed service in every channel, delivered by people who care and know the answers. They prosper because they've built their operation from the perspective of pet parents, earning sales of more than $2 billion, up from just $26 million in 2012.

- Are we accessible to customers, based on their preferences?
- Do we ever put customers on hold for extended periods? Work them through phone trees?
- Do we make customers repeat the information they punched in?
- Do we give our people the answers and ability to help?

#MakeMomProud-O-Meter

OH DEAR. ☐ ☐ ☐ ☐ ☐ SO PROUD!

Do Our Customers Ever Feel Like a Hot Potato?

Are we united in how we serve, without customer handoffs?

Wegmans never wants your mom waiting for someone to get permission to act, nor will they pass her on to someone else for service. They make Mom proud because they train people for their skills and for teamwork. Wegmans even slows their growth until they can hire the right people who can act this way. These actions breed customer admiration and employee retention. Full-time turnover is as low as 4 percent.

- Are our customers ever bounced around in our company?
- Do we ever bounce the customer to partners to solve his or her issue?
- Do we show up as a team to our customer? Are silos united?

#MakeMomProud-O-Meter

OH DEAR. ☐ ☐ ☐ ☐ ☐ SO PROUD!

Would We Send Our Pile of Paperwork to Our Mom?

Do we deliver understanding—not lingo, jargon, and more paper?

USAA insurance decided to clean house on the paperwork trail it requires customers to deal with for every type of process. For example, they reduced the paperwork rigmarole for filing fraudulent credit card charges, reducing paper, process, and time required. This constant focus on making it easier for customers to do business with them continues to earn USAA a 98 percent customer renewal rate.

- Do we ever bombard our customers with paperwork?
- Have we eased the burden of what we require, and how we require it?
- Is our communication clear and understandable—wiped of lingo and jargon?

#MakeMomProud-O-Meter

OH DEAR. ☐ ☐ ☐ ☐ ☐ SO PROUD!

Would Our Customers Say That We "Know" Them?

Do we deliver personal, relevant relationships?

Stitch Fix blends data with humanity and customization. They make Mom proud by automating with data "to a point" and then customizing and personalizing. Finding this blend and balancing it is their prosperity formula. Their business grows, while retail competitors struggle. Delivering a "you know me" experience, driven by data and honed by hand, has led the company to achieve profitability after just six years and sales exceeding $730 million.

- Do our customers feel like we know them?
- Does all of our data connect so we can know and respond to needs?
- Are our people trained and enabled to customize?
- Do our responses, offers, and gestures = "We know you"?

#MakeMomProud-O-Meter

OH DEAR. ☐ ☐ ☐ ☐ ☐ SO PROUD!

"Put Others Before Yourself."

Achieve your goal by helping customers achieve theirs.

Like our moms the Make-mom-proud companies prove with their actions that they have their customers' best interests in mind. This is at the heart of companies that grow most organically—earning ardent admirers who grow their businesses for them. They earn a bigger piece of the pie because they improve customers' lives.

This is a simple idea to accept, but is oh so hard to execute. Operating at this level remains elusive until the paradoxical realization kicks in: To achieve your goals, you need to help others achieve theirs.

"Make Mom Proud" Questions:

Are we improving customers' lives?

Do we achieve our goals through helping our customers achieve theirs?

Do We Have Clarity of Purpose?

Are we all connected in our purpose in improving customers' lives?

IKEA has never wavered from its purpose of "being there for the many people." They make Mom proud by letting people know how it will be to do business with them. And then they unite every silo and every operation so that customers always know what they will and will not get from an IKEA experience. Clarity of purpose drives their prosperity, making them the largest furniture retailer in the world.

- Have we clarified why we exist, our purpose in improving customers' lives?
- Have we translated our purpose to our operation and behaviors, as IKEA does?
- Do we enable employees to deliver on our purpose?

#MakeMomProud-O-Meter

OH DEAR. ☐ ☐ ☐ ☐ ☐ SO PROUD!

Does Our "Hello" Experience Focus on People or Process?

Do we honor customers by starting with their lives, not our action items?

Because Mayfair Diagnostics understands the emotions of the "hello," they redesigned the welcome experience in their imaging clinics. They make Mom proud by looking into the eyes of the people who walk through their door, and they guide—never "process"—the human standing in front of them. Their personalized service welcome, among other gestures, led to accelerated profit for their redesigned clinics.

- Do all of our "hellos" start with honoring the human in front of us?
- Are our interactions first about people or the process and paperwork?
- Do we give our people the time and ability to recognize and welcome?

#MakeMomProud-O-Meter

OH DEAR. ☐ ☐ ☐ ☐ ☐ SO PROUD!

Do We Allow for Human Error?

Does customer empathy exist in our operations, our processes, and our rules?

The make-mom-proud companies stand out with empathetic responses when customers need them. Warby Parker makes Mom proud because they extend grace with every pair of glasses they sell, giving people thirty days to return a pair, even if the customers sat on them. They prosper, earning "goodness-driven growth," primarily through word of mouth, and these practices that are part of their regular "operating procedure."

· Do we allow a little wiggle room for human error by customers?
· Have we enabled our employees to extend grace when they see fit?
· Do we understand vulnerable customer moments, and design services and gestures to support them?

#MakeMomProud-O-Meter

OH DEAR. ☐ ☐ ☐ ☐ ☐ SO PROUD!

Have We Earned a Place in the Story of Customers' Lives?

Are we improving lives in the experience we deliver?

When you focus on adding value to people's lives, they will remember you. The Girl Scouts of Greater New York decided to benefit the lives of homeless girls by offering the benefits of scouting to them. They make Mom proud because they selflessly found a way to fund, create, and sustain this experience that these girls will carry with them for the rest of their lives.

· Have we identified a few experiences we want to be remembered for?
· Across our customer journey, does everyone in our organization unite to deliver?
· Do we design in memories as part of these experiences we deliver?

#MakeMomProud-O-Meter

OH DEAR. ☐ ☐ ☐ ☐ ☐ SO PROUD!

Do We Understand Customer Emotions?

Do we design experiences to earn positive emotional responses?

The Starlight Children's Foundation found a whole new version of that nutty hospital gown, inspired by giving sick teens back the identity they lost in the standard-issue gown. They make Mom proud by not only acknowledging the emotion of these kids, but also by taking action to turn a negative to a positive. They deliver prosperity by improving the lives of more than sixty million sick kids in the United States, Canada, Australia, and the UK.

· Do we understand our customers' emotions as they work with us?
· Do we use this understanding to redesign existing experiences?
· Do we use this understanding to innovate new experiences?

#MakeMomProud-O-Meter

OH DEAR. ☐ ☐ ☐ ☐ ☐ SO PROUD!

Do We Walk Customers Out of Trouble Spots?

Would our customers say that we "have" them when things go wrong?

Alaska Airlines has prepared everyone to take action when it's their customers' time for a Murphy's Law travel day. They make Mom proud by providing all employees with tool kits and sets of actions they can use to help customers out of tough situations—without asking permission. When customers are taken care of, prosperity follows; Alaska Airlines is frequently named best airline in the United States, according to many industry indices.

· Have we proactively identified regular customer trouble spots?
· Have we designed solutions that employees can take immediately?
· Do we reward behavior to make customers whole again?

#MakeMomProud-O-Meter

OH DEAR. ☐ ☐ ☐ ☐ ☐ SO PROUD!

Do We Dare Rethink What's *Always* Been Done?

Are we redesigning experiences based on customers' needs and lives?

The Dorchester Collection realized that by understanding their guests' attachment to their wardrobes and its importance in their lives, their laundry service was completely out of sync. They make Mom proud because they did not rest until their garment-care experience was redesigned to meet their guest goals for upkeep and preservation.

· Across our customer journey, are we clear about all customer goals?
· Have we oriented what we deliver, and how to meet them?
· Do customer goals drive innovation in products, service, and operations?
· Do we continue any practices because "that's how they've always been done"?

#MakeMomProud-O-Meter

OH DEAR. ☐ ☐ ☐ ☐ ☐ SO PROUD!

Do We Give Customers Choices That Jibe with Their Lives?

Do we cater to customer preferences as we deliver to them?

Sephora knows what their customers want, and they know all of the different versions for how customers like to receive goods and service. They make Mom proud because they respect all of these needs, translating them into multiple options for service, sales, experiences, and communication. Their more than ten million zealous customers repay Sephora by returning to them again and again.

· Do we actively give customers choices in how to interact with us?
· Are we delivering relevant communications?
· Do we make it easy for customers to engage with us as they choose?

#MakeMomProud-O-Meter

OH DEAR. ☐ ☐ ☐ ☐ ☐ SO PROUD!

"Take the High Road."

Choose how you will and will not grow.

The make-mom-proud companies are choosing to reverse the trend on business practices that have defined their industries. Through leadership guidance and company actions, they are establishing more balanced relationships, where both sides win. Both customer and company are better off because they are in each other's lives.

"Make Mom Proud" Questions:

Do we take the high road?

Are we deliberate and steady in what we will, and will not do, to grow?

Do Leaders Inspire What They Want Delivered?

Do we align what we stand for with how we act?

REI's purpose is to get folks outdoors. Consistent with that purpose, they close their doors on Black Friday, urging families and friends to be together and head out. REI makes Mom proud because they deliberately take risks to grow differently than business as usual. Their clear purpose and aligned actions are magnets for attracting and keeping valued employees. REI has been on *Fortune*'s 100 Best Companies to Work For list for nineteen consecutive years.

· Like the CEO of REI, do our leaders bring our purpose to life?
· Are employees involved in defining actions that define our purpose?
· Do we *live* our purpose with our actions and behaviors?

#MakeMomProud-O-Meter

OH DEAR. ☐ ☐ ☐ ☐ ☐ SO PROUD!

Are We Honoring Customers as Assets?

Do we remember and value customers, and not take them for granted?

Bonobos takes the science of knowing and caring for their best customers seriously. They make Mom proud because their good customers are never taken for granted and never forgotten. They combine the science of knowing them and the art of service and experience to earn continued growth and increased lifetime value of new customers by 20 percent.

· Like Bonobos, do we know and manage customer lifetime value?
· Do we enable the front line to know customers' value, so they can decide on actions?
· Are we taking actions to honor our best customers?
· Do we do anything for new customers that we don't do for our best customers?

#MakeMomProud-O-Meter

OH DEAR. ☐ ☐ ☐ ☐ ☐ SO PROUD!

Does Two-way Trust Define Our Actions?

Do we earn customer trust by trusting them back?

Lemonade Insurance wanted to remove the imbalance that sometimes defines the insurance experience. They make Mom proud because they have built processes that have trust as their foundation. For example, their claims process includes an honesty pledge, where they choose to believe customers' words. Prosperity follows, as customers gravitate to them for this foundation of trust.

· Do we practice two-way trust with customers?
· Have we created a customer relationship where both sides win?
· Do customers feel that we trust them through the language in our forms, our fine print, and as they work through our paperwork and contracts?

#MakeMomProud-O-Meter

OH DEAR.   ☐   ☐   ☐   ☐   ☐   SO PROUD!

Do We Have Any "Gotcha!" Moments?

Can we deliver "We've got your back" moments instead?

The Columbus Metropolitan Library decided to walk away from the "Gotcha!" experience of overdue fines. They make Mom proud because, with this act, they decided to stay true to their mission to help young minds grow and let people learn. The first major library in the United States to do this, they are creating a movement of "good-habit libraries" to keep people reading rather than worrying about those fines.

· Do we have any "if," "and," or "but" conditions in our experience?
· Do customers experience any surprises in conditions on products, services, fees, or offers?
· Are we working to flip "Gotcha!" moments to "We've got your back" moments?

#MakeMomProud-O-Meter

OH DEAR.   ☐   ☐   ☐   ☐   ☐   SO PROUD!

Are There Any "Gullibility Tax" Situations in Our Business?

Do we share all the facts, so customers can decide?

Luscious Garage in San Francisco turned the experience of getting a car repaired from one of fear and worry to one of honor and trust. They make Mom proud with completely transparent information, communication, and options that breed a partnership between technician and customer. And no "gullibility tax" ever. Always honestly giving customers facts, choice, and a say in the matter has earned them nothing but five-star reviews.

- Do we have "gullibility moments" in our experience?
- Do any customers ever feel like they've been oversold?
- Are customers guided fearlessly to the right options for them?
- Do our rewards encourage selling what's best for the customer?

#MakeMomProud-O-Meter

OH DEAR. ☐ ☐ ☐ ☐ ☐ SO PROUD!

Do We Ever Practice Nickeling and Diming, or Opportunity Pricing?

Are we charging what's fair, not what's possible?

Virgin Hotels decided to walk away from the practice of overcharging customers at the mini bar—just because they could. They make Mom proud because fairness rules how they price and what they practice. Charging the same price as you can get down the street at the market, and other fair habits, hoisted them to the number one spot on Condé Nast Traveler Readers' Choice Awards for the United States.

- Do we practice any nickeling and diming to customers?
- Are we becoming dependent on these fees and charges to grow financially?
- Do we do the work to eliminate these practices from our business?

#MakeMomProud-O-Meter

OH DEAR. ☐ ☐ ☐ ☐ ☐ SO PROUD!

Is Our Apology Our Finest Hour?

Do we show our humanity and put customers back together again?

Every day and after every shift, Four Seasons teams identify any glitches that might have occurred with customers. They make Mom proud because the focus is on the "why," not on the "who." Through digging into causes, getting rid of them, and letting the front line solve those glitches, content employees prosper, putting the company on the *Forbes* 100 Best Places to Work list for eighteen years straight.

· Like the Four Seasons, do we know what customer glitches occur every day?
· Do we have a recovery plan prepared that kicks into place when big mistakes happen?
· Do we guide and enable employees to take ownership and remove them?

#MakeMomProud-O-Meter

OH DEAR. ☐ ☐ ☐ ☐ ☐ SO PROUD!

Are Truth and Transparency How We Sell and Serve?

Do we focus on earning the relationship, not making the sale?

OVO Energy decided that they wanted to show up like a trusted friend in how they sell and serve. They make Mom proud by making sure prices reflect the actual cost of doing business so customers always know and feel that they're getting a good deal. This is driving their growth and trust among consumers, where they are rated 8.8/10 by Trustpilot, a new high for energy.

· Do we always deliver transparency in how we price and what customers receive?
· Is our selling experience uncomplicated and clear?
· Is our pricing easy to understand?
· Would customers describe their experience with us as truthful and transparent?

#MakeMomProud-O-Meter

OH DEAR. ☐ ☐ ☐ ☐ ☐ SO PROUD!

Now... It's Up to You.

Use This Book to Decide How You Will, and Will Not, Grow to #MakeMomProud.

The stories of the make-mom-proud companies in this book gave you a view of decisions and actions they took to earn customer and employee admiration and growth. As you progressed through each chapter, understanding their decisions, and then contrasting them to your own, you should now know how different or similar your actions and decisions are to theirs.

The decisions you make in business measure the depth of your humanity: your ability to apply that simple Golden Rule. How you choose to correct something that goes wrong, how steadfast you are in delivering the goods—ensuring quality and giving people what they need to do these things—expose what you value. The actions that flow from these decisions expose the kind of people you are. When you honor your customers and employees, they tell your story for you. They become the army that markets your products and services every day around the world.

We all know that love is irrational. Customer love is a reward for what some consider *irrational* business behavior. The make-mom-proud companies get a disproportionate piece of the pie because they aren't always looking over their shoulder at what each decision will get them. They choose to grow by taking actions in business that line up with actions they'd take at home, with their mom.

So make a choice. With each shipment you make, with each tweet, with every hello and good-bye, with each good moment and every challenging one, make a choice about how you want to show up in the marketplace. Decide how you want customers and employees to define who you are and what you value, based on the behaviors you bring to work with you. Making it happen begins with how you choose to grow. Are you ready?

"Call your mother. Tell her you love her. Remember, you're the only person who knows what her heart sounds like from the inside."

–RACHEL WOLCHIN

7.

Join the Movement to #MakeMomProud.

This is a book with a funny title, but a very earnest mission.
And that is to improve our lives as customers.

We all have it in us to take actions to "Make Mom Proud." Yet our lives as customers are still filled with some squishy experiences we'd rather not have had.

The goal of this movement is to boost us up by taking actions, one at a time, and then sharing them with each other. This work is one-step-at-a-time work. And so is this movement. One action will lead to another, and then another, and then another.

You Have the Fixings to #MakeMomProud

So first, we invite you to honor your mom at make-mom-proud.com by **posting your mom's picture** and a description of an action you've taken in business that makes the lives of customers or employees better. While you're there, you can see what others have done, see their moms' faces, and compare stories.

Here's where we will buoy each other, celebrate progress, and keep taking those steps to move forward. And we will feature your progress on social media and on our blog so that we can all celebrate your success.

Post Your Progress at Make-mom-proud.com

Next, in social media, let the marketplace know you're improving customers' lives by using the hashtag #MakeMomProud. We learn and grow from each other, by standing on the shoulders of the people who came before us. We learn by fearlessly sharing our foibles, our journeys, our joys, and our successes.

To advance all of us in making this a movement, share the acts you take as you progress on social media using the hashtag #MakeMomProud. Share what you're doing and why the act you've taken is part of your march toward becoming a make-mom-proud company.

I wish you joy, success, and contentment in your road ahead.

As always, reach out if you ever need a hand in urging you on!

Jeanne Bliss

It is my pleasure to share the interviews, references, and source notes that contributed to this book's content and made it possible. Please go to http://www.customerbliss.com/books, where you can also access tools and the videos and comics from this book.

Gratitude

Well, it's done. Book four. What you hold in your hands is my "thank you" for letting my words into your life.

I'm grateful to our community of brave customer crusaders from every kind of business across the globe. Charging up that hill together is the honor of my professional life. Getting to know you, and your passion, and your journey, and your ups and downs while doing this work is a privilege. And to learn from you that in my own small way, I have helped—that is joy to me. Your partnership and friendship and generosity stir my enthusiasm for this work, even after these thirty-five years of being dedicated to *only* this work.

I'm grateful for the bumps and stumbles and the scrapes that I've experienced as a customer experience practitioner, because without them, I honestly could not have written this book for you. And weirdly, I'm grateful for the ups and downs I've had in my life as a customer. These experiences bind us all together in the human condition of being a customer, and the necessity of drawing upon those experiences to serve them.

Thank you to Leah, and Helen and Will and Adrian and Alyssa at Portfolio for believing in me once again! Zontee and Brandyce, our partnership is so important. Mark and team and Ken and team—my optimism for what we can do together with this "mom book" holds no bounds!

To my husband, Bill, I'd need to thank you constantly to express my gratitude for taking this journey with me. Grateful that you don't need that, I am, however, most grateful for your "crazy good support" when I am writing. You deserve some kind of husband award. For Linda and Lydia, you are both in my heart every day. Thank you. Finally, to my dad, who is never far from my thoughts, I send thanks wherever you are. And to Mom, I hope as your daughter that I #MakeMomProud.

Index